BUILT FOR GREATNESS

81 Ways To Unleash Your Inner Power
For Purposeful Living

Christian Edition of the Tao Te Ching

Keith D. Hoang

Archbishop Sylvain Lavoie, OMI

Contents

We cannot all do great things, but we can do small things with great love.

— St. Mother Teresa

Introduction

What Is Built For Greatness?

How many self-help or life-strategy books do you know have been around for thousands of years and are still revered by millions of people today? If there were such books, would you agree they would contain a powerful message regarding how we should live our lives? And what if it turned out the essential principles these books promoted were much the same? I believe there are two such books: the Bible and the Tao Te Ching. This book features a text of the Tao Te Ching infused with language from the Bible to clarify themes common to both books. It reveals profound spiritual principles that, when put into practice, can set you on your own personal spiritual journey: finding, orienting yourself toward and then following the flow of God's Spirit in your life, trusting it to guide your actions and amplify your efforts so you can achieve your best possible life.

At first glance, you might think the Bible and the ancient Chinese book the Tao Te Ching would have little in common. As a lifelong Catholic, I certainly thought so for most of my life—or would have, if I had given the topic any thought. After all, the Bible and the Tao Te Ching come from different times and different cultures. The Bible is primarily a religious book, while the Tao Te Ching isn't religious at all. The Bible is some three-quarters of a million words long and would take weeks (or longer) to read in its entirety, while the Tao Te Ching contains only 81 brief chapters and can be read in a single afternoon.

My own personal journey has brought me to a place where I see the Bible and the Tao Te Ching *do* have much in common. In fact, as I see it, God's truth as revealed in the Bible also flows through the Tao Te Ching in the form of principles—some might even say *spiritual* principles—that, when put into practice, can help you achieve your goals without wasted effort, experience serenity whatever your circumstances, and otherwise improve your life, sometimes dramatically.

Just what are these principles? To my mind, one of the most powerful is what the Bible might call "living in the Spirit"—that is, praying to understand God's will, putting forth effort to accomplish it and (this is crucial) *trusting* that as you cooperate with the Spirit, the Spirit will add God's energy to your endeavors, so you can actually accomplish more with less work. The Tao Te Ching has a similar, paradoxical teaching called *wei wu wei*, which can be described as "action without action." It refers to the idea that when you cooperate with the Tao, or the Way of the universe, your efforts are magnified, and you achieve results better than those you could ever achieve solely through your own initiative.

Another principle found in both the Bible and the Tao Te Ching is learning to live in the moment without undue concern about what the future might bring. This goes against our nature in this day and age. We always seem to be planning, striving, trying to attain possessions, security, and peace of mind. Learning to be content in the present moment with whatever we may or may not have seems … unproductive. And yet, as both of these wise books affirm, staying grounded in the moment isn't necessarily mere passivity; instead, if done mindfully, it can be an abiding trust that God is working for our good and will give us all we need (as a student of the Bible might put it), or that we are living in harmony with the Tao and we do not need what we currently do not have (as a student of the Tao Te Ching might put it).

This Christian edition of the Tao Te Ching is like a road map helping us realize we are Built For Greatness. On this path, "greatness" isn't about putting forth maximum effort to achieve fame, financial success or other such trappings that the world commonly venerates. Rather, as mentioned above, Built For Greatness is about finding, orienting yourself toward and then following the flow of energy and God's Spirit in your life, trusting it both to guide your actions and to amplify your efforts to achieve your best possible life. This might include wealth and other material blessings; or it might not. Everyone's path is different. The key is to find your journey and follow it, trusting it to take you where it will. If you take care of the journey, the destination will take care of itself.

Why the Tao Te Ching?

The title of the Tao Te Ching can be translated "Book of the Tao and Virtue," "Book of the Way and Its Virtue" or "The Way and the Power." According to tradition, it was written by a sage named Lao Tzu (or Old Master), who was a renowned scholar and a record-keeper at the royal court of China's Zhou Dynasty during the 6th century BCE.

In today's religious forms of Taoism, some revere Lao Tzu as a divine being, while others argue that he is strictly a mythical figure. Scholars still debate the text's true authorship, with many contending that "Lao Tzu" was actually a collection of various authors. But the debate over the Tao Te Ching's authorship does not diminish its power and insight. Its 81 brief chapters consist of short poems, which range from political wisdom for kings and leaders to practical advice for everyday people. It is probably the most influential Chinese book of all time, and it may have been translated into English more times than any other Chinese document. Many believe it is the most famous and influential of all Taoist texts that teaches one undivided truth at the root of all things.

The text of the Tao Te Ching is divided into two parts. The first (chapters 1–37) concerns the Tao, which is the way of the universe, the source of life, and the power in all nature. It exceeds our senses, thoughts, and imagination, and if it were to reveal itself in all its fullness and glory, humanity would not be able to bear the vision. These early chapters explain how we can orient our lives to this way of the universe.

The second part of the Tao Te Ching gives further details about "Te" (chapters 38–81), which means virtue or power. "Te" is the energy that can be cultivated by a person through living harmoniously with the Tao. Together, the Tao Te Ching can be called the Way of Power, or, in other words, the Way of God by the Power of the Holy Spirit.

I am a Christian practicing as a Catholic, so I understand that these concepts might sound strange or peculiar to many Christian ears. But I believe deeply they contain and help reveal the wisdom of God—the same wisdom of God that is found in the Bible. After researching and studying over fifty leading authors of the Tao Te Ching, I utilized words from a Christian context with the same meaning, and chose Christian scriptures that parallel to the Tao Te Ching. In so doing, I hope to help Christians and non-Christians alike to see that God's wisdom as contained in the Bible also flows through the Tao Te Ching, for I believe that without God, the Tao Te Ching would not exist as one of the wisest books ever written.

How Do I Read This Book?

Although the Tao Te Ching can easily be read in just a few hours, the text becomes much more powerful when it is read slowly, mentally digested through patient prayer and meditation, and its principles actually put into practice. The richness of the Tao Te Ching is a lifelong exploration of discovering something new about yourself every time you read it.

For these reasons, I suggest you avoid the temptation to rush through this book. Instead, try reading just one chapter every day in a kind of 81-day experiment. First find a place to read that is free from distractions. Then, approaching the text with a heart open to change, read a single chapter the Tao, and the Bible verses related to it. Be sure to spend time in prayer and meditation after you read; otherwise the lessons are too easily forgotten in the course of the day. Many people find it helpful to keep a journal of their thoughts, both to help them retain what they've learned and to serve as a handy reference later. Finally, look for opportunities during your day-to-day life to try out the principles you will be discovering. You will be pleasantly surprised at how quickly they bear fruit.

At the end of your 81 days and the 81 chapters, take a spiritual inventory. How have your thoughts changed over the last eleven weeks? What are you doing differently now? Do you have an increased sense of peace and stillness in your life? As you continue to explore these new ideas, you very well might find yourself repeating this 81-day experiment.

God has worked many miracles in bringing this book to fruition, and writing it has truly been a labor of love on my part, as it nearly consumed my normal life for five years. I pray that in reading it, you too will be drawn closer to God—for when we are One with God in Spirit, we are truly Built For Greatness. Amen!

My Journey

I am a father of 5 beautiful children married to a very supportive wife, Tracy. I immigrated to the United States in 1975 from Vietnam and currently live in Los Angeles, California. My call to serve God started in 1999, but it was in 2007 when our Holy Mother Mary appeared to me with a clear message. I surrendered and found myself praying the rosary and asking for forgiveness. I heard the voice of Mary calling me to St. Vincent de Paul Church in downtown Los Angeles where I met Richard, a homeless man who taught me the Bible for three months. His understanding of the Bible is beyond mystical, but even greater is Richard's love for our Holy Mother Mary. After our last meeting, I was inspired to create a Christian version of the Tao Te Ching and sent a manuscript to Dr. Michael Downey, a professor at St. John Seminary and the editor of the award-winning The New Dictionary of Catholic Spirituality. He shared with me the importance of such a book, especially in China.

In 2012, I completed a first Christian version of the Tao Te Ching. God promised to call His faithful representative of the Catholic Church to help me send His message written in the book to the world. An almost miraculous intervention led me to meet Archbishop Emeritus Sylvain Lavoie OMI who accepted to help me promote the book, and eventually became co-author. He shared with me the journey in my life is very much like the book of Job. It wasn't until February 2017, we met Archbishop José H. Gómez and Fr. Brian Nunes (secretary of the LA Archdiocese to Archbishop José H. Gómez) who gave me their blessings to support my mission. I knew the angels where celebrating when I received a letter from Archbishop José H. Gómez who wrote, "Be assured of my prayers for you and your intentions, and I ask that you keep me in yours as well. May Jesus, through the intercession of Mary, grant you a blessed Easter Season."

Along this journey, I asked God, "Why me?" This led me to learn about my family. My father shared with me my great-great grandfather, Hoang Lenh Thu died a martyr for the faith and my great grandfather and grandmother Riem built a Catholic Church in North Vietnam, Phuong Duc. Next to this beautiful church is a burial site built for them in remembrance of their devotion to God. My mission became clearer when I learned my father and his siblings helped rebuild churches in Vietnam and the U.S. I told my father it looks like God is working in my life with all the prayers and blessings of the family to continue building the Kingdom of God. The two saints who always remind me to keep going are St. Francis of Assisi and St. Mother Teresa of Calcutta.

Thus began my five-year journey of biblical and spiritual study to complete the first Christian version of the Tao Te Ching. God shared with me the Tao Te Ching will serve as a bridge to God's throne of mercy to find grace in the battle field of the wounded. It is this initial encounter between a sinner and amazing grace that will unify people from different origins of the world regardless of their religion, skin color, and title. The principles are ever more important today, teaching us to keep our priorities clear so we can follow the Spirit of God and exercise leadership with God's amazing grace. It is this Spirit that triumphs in the hearts of the people to begin building new bridges between the Church and God's people, both East and West.

In the wake of a Reformation dividing Christianity 500 years ago, I believe this Christian version of the Tao Te Ching will be vital as a unifying spiritual Reformation. My prayer is for the church to recognize the importance of spreading the gospel using the foundational principles of the Tao Te Ching spirituality contained in this book to build the Kingdom of God.

Preface

An Improbable, Remarkable Journey

You may be asking yourself, how did an emeritus archbishop from Canada ever get involved in co-authoring a book on the Tao Te Ching?

The answer is as improbable and mysterious as the existence of the book itself, and in that sense begging to be included with this work, so here it is, as a preface.

Keith Hoang introduced himself to me after one of my presentations at the Los Angeles Religious Education Congress in 2017. He had intended to take another workshop, but for some strange reason, kept being directed by a security person into mine.

Keith felt inspired to introduce himself to me, described his venture into writing The Path To Greatness and asked if I could help him promote it within the Church. He spoke with such conviction and excitement about its possibility in terms of inter-religious dialogue I could not help but be interested and agreed to do what I could. Ultimately, he wanted to meet Pope Francis whom he felt would be interested in this project.

Upon my return to Canada, I received from Keith a rather unique (for me) electronic version of the book consisting of a chapter of the Tao Te Ching text on each page with the related scripture references on the bottom. That arrangement did not really appeal to me and I let it lie dormant until further correspondence with Keith prompted me to take some initiative. I contacted the Apostolic Nunciature in Ottawa about the book and they suggested Keith work through his local bishop, who happened to be Archbishop José Gomez of Los Angeles.

I knew Archbishop Gomez because of the dinners he hosted for the bishops during the Religious Education Congress each year. Still, I was hesitant to bother him with the question of the book and again let things be. However, I was planning a writing-vacation at Our Lady of Mt. Carmel Parish in Newport Beach in January 2018, and suggested to Keith we could meet while I was there. He informed me in the meantime he had met the archbishop's assistant, Fr. Brian Nunes, and asked me to try to arrange a meeting with the archbishop through him. Again, I was hesitant and did not act on that suggestion.

When we met in January, I realized how devastated Keith felt because of my lack of action on his behalf, and my lack of appreciation of the five years and personal cost writing the book had demanded of him. With that motivation, I made the phone call, an appointment was arranged, and we found ourselves meeting with Archbishop Gomez and Fr. Nunes for an exciting visit that went well over the allotted time.

When Archbishop Gomez expressed both interest and support for the project, I suggested the book needed to be revised into a more developed format placing the scripture references partially written out on the opposite page to each chapter of the Tao Te Ching. Keith immediately agreed, and asked if I could do that.

Hesitating to take on more work as I was in the process of writing a book of my own, yet also feeling some lingering guilt at my lack of immediate action to Keith's first request, I replied I would, but only after completing my book. Upon further reflection, however, I realized as the work involved scripture, perhaps I could incorporate revising the book into my morning prayer as part of the Office of Readings, replacing the second reading I would have already read numerous times. That plan proved to be quite satisfactory and so the task of revising the book, one chapter every couple of days, began even before I completed my own writing task.

As I prayed through the text and the scriptures, it dawned on me the journey down to California that January with my car carrying my scooter on a Versahaul and pulling a trailer with my two sailboards and a kayak was actually a metaphor for the revision of the book.

Travelling alone through the slowly receding snow for three days and three thousand kilometers through the rugged, barren, windswept, beautiful States of Montana, Idaho, Utah, Arizona and Nevada to California was exciting and captivating, much like journeying through the Tao Te Ching for the first time and about which I knew very little.

Returning home by the same route proved to be just as interesting as the trip down, as everything was now seen from a different perspective. That trip was like journeying through the very familiar Christian scriptures, only this time through the prism of the Tao Te Ching, revealing exciting and inspiring connections all along the way.

After returning home, I purchased a larger scooter, and faced the challenge of how to transport it on my next trip to the States. The folks at the local dealership I consulted informed me it was both remarkable and improbable I made it to my destination with that Versahaul, as I was scraping the highway with every major bump. Therein lay the title for this preface – both journeys were remarkable and improbable – the physical travelling to California and my eventual safe arrival, and the meeting up with Keith and the literary, spiritual revision of *The Path To Greatness* that has evolved into *Built For Greatness*.

Who knows – maybe the culmination of both ventures may result in another remarkable, improbable journey – meeting with Pope Francis to share this whole story with him.

KEITH D. HOANG, B.S. BIOLOGY
HANSONELLIS.COM CO-FOUNDER,
SPIRITUAL PUBLIC SPEAKER,
AND AUTHOR. KEITH IS AN AWARD
WINNING WEB DESIGNER AND
ENTREPRENEUR RECOGNIZED
FOR HIS BUSINESS LEADERSHIP
AND ONLINE SUCCESS IN THE
CITY OF TORRANCE AND REDONDO
BEACH, CALIFORNIA. HE IS INVOLVED IN MULTIPLE NON-PROFIT
FOUNDATIONS TO HELP THE FUTURE OF YOUNG CHILDREN, THE
POOR, AND MENTALLY ILL. KEITH IS PASSIONATE ABOUT SHARING
HIS FAITH AT BUSINESS CONFERENCES. HE ENJOYS SPENDING
TIME WITH HIS WIFE AND BEST FRIEND OF 30 YEARS AND THEIR
FIVE CHILDREN. KEITH IS INSPIRED BY MOTHER TERESA OF
CALCUTTA AND ST. FRANCIS OF ASSISI.

ARCHBISHOP SYLVAIN LAVOIE, O.M.I.
HE IS A MEMBER OF THE MISSIONARY
OBLATES OF MARY IMMACULATE WHO
HAS SPENT OVER 35 YEARS
MINISTERING AMONG THE INDIGENOUS
PEOPLES OF NORTHERN
SASKATCHEWAN AND MANITOBA,
CANADA. HE SERVED AS ARCHBISHOP

OF KEEWATIN-LE PAS UNTIL 2011 AND NOW SERVES AS CHAPLAIN
AND SPIRITUAL DIRECTOR AT STAR OF THE NORTH RETREAT
CENTRE IN ST. ALBERT, ALBERTA. AUTHOR OF FOUR BOOKS,
ARCHBISHOP LAVOIE OFFERS RETREATS AND WORKSHOPS
THROUGHOUT NORTH AMERICA ON INDIGENOUS MINISTRY,
SPIRITUALITY, FORGIVENESS, GRIEVING, PERSONAL HEALING,
ADDICTIONS AWARENESS AND THE TWELVE STEP PROGRAM.

B U I L T   F O R   G R E A T N E S S

81 Ways To Unleash Your Inner Power
For Purposeful Living

Christian Edition of the Tao Te Ching

Chapter 1
Mystery of God

If you can talk about it [a]
It is not the Eternal God

If you can name it [b]
It is not the Eternal Name

The nameless, is the origin of Heaven and Earth [c]

The nameable, is the mother of all things [d]

Free from desire, one observes the Spirit [e]
Filled with desire, one observes the flesh

The two emerge and become one of the same body [f]
    but differ in name
The unity is the Mystery of God
Mystery of mysteries
The gateway to wonders

[a] John 17:25 *("Righteous Father, the world does not know you, but I know you; and these know that you have sent me.)*
Matthew 11:27, Job 36:26, Job 37:5, 1 John 4:7-19, Luke 6:45

[b] Judges 13:18 *(But the angel of the Lord said to him, "Why do you ask my name? It is too wonderful.")*
Exodus 3:13-15

[c] Genesis 1:1-2 *(In the beginning when God created the heavens and the earth, the earth was a formless void and darkness covered the face of the deep, while a wind from God swept over the face of the waters.)*

[d] Genesis 3:20 *(The man named his wife Eve, because she was the mother of all living.)*

[e] Romans 8:9-18 *(But you are not in the flesh; you are in the Spirit, since the Spirit of God dwells in you...)*

[f] Ephesians 4:4-6 *(There is one body and one Spirit, just as you were called to the one hope of your calling, one Lord, one faith, one baptism, one God and Father of all, who is above all and through all and in all.)*
1 Corinthians 12:12-14, 1 Corinthians 6:19

Chapter 2
Dualities

If beauty is recognized in the world [a]
Then ugliness arises
If good is recognized in the world [b]
Then bad arises

Spirit and flesh form each other
Difficult and easy produce each other
Long and short measure each other
High and low define each other
Music and tone harmonize each other
Front and back follow each other

Therefore, the Son of God: [c]
Achieves His purpose but not by His own actions [d]
Conveys the teachings but not by His own words
Holds all things together but not by controlling
Creates all but does not possess
Serves all but does not seek glory
Fulfills the promise to all but does not claim it
Since He does not claim anything
Nothing is ever lost

[a] 1 Peter 3:3-5 *(Do not adorn yourselves outwardly by braiding your hair, and by wearing gold ornaments or fine clothing; rather, let your adornment be the inner self with the lasting beauty of a gentle and quiet spirit, which is very precious in God's sight. It was in this way long ago that the holy women who hoped in God used to adorn themselves by accepting the authority of their husbands.)*

[b] Job 30:26 *(But when I looked for good, evil came; and when I waited for light, darkness came.)*
Ecclesiastes 9:1-3, Galatians 5:16-26

[c] Matthew 3:13-17 *(…"This is my son, the Beloved, in whom I am well pleased.")*
Mark 3:11, Luke 22:70, John 10:22-36, Acts 13:34

[d] Colossians 1:15-23 *(He is the image of the invisible God, the first born of all creation; for in him all thing in heaven and on earth were created, things visible and invisible, whether thrones or dominions or rulers or powers - all things have been created through him and for him…)*
John 5:19-20, John 14:10

Chapter 3

Renewal

If we do not regard powerful men highly [a]
People will not fight for power
If we do not value rare goods [b]
People will not become thieves
If we display desirable things [c]
We bring confusion in our hearts

Thus, one who is with the Spirit leads by: [d]
Clearing our minds under the law
And renewing our hearts under grace
Weakening our selfish ambition [e]
And strengthening our core with love

The Spirit steers us away from our desires [f]
So those who cleverly scheme have no power over us

Be still [g]
And everything will be in order

[a] James 2:5-7 *(Listen, my beloved brothers and sisters. Has not God chosen the poor in the world to be rich in faith and to be heirs of the kingdom that he has promised to those who love him?)*
Matthew 5:3

[b] 1 Timothy 6:6-10 *(...Of course there is great gain in godliness combined with contentment; for we brought nothing into the world, so that we can take nothing out of it; but if we have food and clothing, we will be content with these...)*

[c] Matthew 23:27-28 *("Woe to you, scribes and Pharisees, hypocrites! For you are like whitewashed tombs, which on the outside look beautiful, but on the inside are full of the bones of the dead and of all kinds of filth...)*
Romans 8:18-27

[d] Romans 6:14 *(For sin will have no dominion over you, since you are not under law, but under grace.)*
Romans 7:4-6, Romans 7:14-25, Galatians 3:10-14, Galatians 5:13-25

[e] Philippians 2:1-8 *(...Let the same mind be in you that was in Christ Jesus, who, though he was in the form of God, did not regard equality with God as something to be exploited, but emptied himself, taking the form of a slave...)*

[f] Romans 13:14 *(Instead, put on the Lord Jesus Christ, and make no provisions for the flesh, to gratify its desires.)*
Galatians 5:17

[g] Psalm 37:7-15 *(Be still before the Lord, and wait patiently for him; do not fret over those who prosper in their way, over those who carry out evil deeds.)*

Chapter 4
Nature of God

The Way is limitless [a]
Used by everyone but never filled up

So unfathomable!
The infinite source of all things created

It blunts the sharp edges
Unravels the entanglements
Harmonizes the light
And unites the dust of the Earth

Invisible, but always present [b]
You may ask whose child it is [c]
I say He is the Son of the Living God before existence

[a] John 14:4-6 *(And you know the way to the place where I am going."*
Thomas said to him, "Lord, we do not know where you are going. How can
we know the way?" Jesus said to him, "I am the way, and the truth, and the
life. No one comes to the Father except through me.)
Genesis 2:1-9, Romans 11:33-34, Isaiah 40:13-14,
1 Corinthians 2:1

[b] Colossians 1:15-20 *(He is the image of the invisible God, the first born of*
all creation; for in him all things in heaven and on earth were create, things
visible and invisible…)
John 14:20

[c] Matthew 16:13-20

(Now when Jesus came into the district of Caesarea Philippi, he asked his
disciples, "Who do people say that the Son of Man is?" And they said,
"Some say John the Baptist, but others Elijah, and still others Jeremiah or
one of the prophets." He said to them, "But who do you say that I am?"
Simon Peter answered, "You are the Messiah, the Son of the living God.")
Mark 8:27-29

Chapter 5
Being Impartial

Heaven and Earth do not take sides [a]
They let both the righteous and unrighteous exist
The Son of Man does not take sides [b]
He loves both His neighbors and His enemies

The space between Heaven and Earth is an inexhaustible source:
Empty, yet infinitely capable of all things [c]
With the measure you use [d]
It will be measured to you and even more

Too many words result in failure [e]
It is better to keep silent

[a] 1 Peter 3:18 *(For Christ also suffered for sins, once for all, the righteous for the unrighteous, in order to bring you to God...)*

[b] Matthew 5:43-45 *("You have heard that it was said, "You shall love your neighbor and hate your enemy.' But I say to you, Love your enemies and pray for those who persecute you, so that you may be children of your Father in heaven; for he makes his sun rise on the evil and on the good, and sends rain on the righteous and on the unrighteous.)*
Matthew 20:28

[c] Matthew 19:26 *(But Jesus looked at them and said, "For mortals it is impossible, but with God all things are possible.")*

[d] Mark 4:24-25 *(And he said to them, "Pay attention to what you hear; the measure you give will be the measure you get, and still more will be given you. For to those who have, more will be given; and from those who have nothing, even what they have will be taken away.")*

[e] Proverbs 10:19 *(When words are many, transgression is not lacking, but the prudent are restrained in speech.)*
Job 35:16, Proverbs 17:27-28, James 1:26-27

Chapter 6
The Living Spirit

The Spirit of God is everlasting [a]
It is called the Supreme Creator

The gateway of the Mystic Creator [b]
Is called the source of Heaven and Earth

This power flows continuously [c]
It seems hidden within us
Utilize it, it will not grow tired or weary [a]

[a] Isaiah 40:28-31 *(Have you not known? Have you not heard? The Lord is the everlasting God, the Creator of the ends of the earth. He does not grow faint or weary; his understanding is unsearchable. He gives power to the frail and strengthens the powerless. Even youths will faint and be weary, and the young will fall exhausted; but those who wait for the Lord shall renew their strength, they shall mount up with wings like eagles, they shall run and not be weary, they shall walk and not faint.)*
Genesis 1:2, Ephesians 3:7, Ephesians 3:14-21

[b] Colossians 1:15-16 *(He is the image of the invisible God, the firstborn of all creation; for in him all things in heaven and on earth were created, things visible and invisible, whether thrones or dominions or rulers or powers - all things have been created through him and for him.)*

[c] John 14:20 *(On that day you will know that I am in my Father, and you in me and I in you.)*
1 Corinthians 6:19

Chapter 7
The Sacrifice

The Heavens and Earth are everlasting [a]
How can the Heavens and Earth last forever?
Because they do not exist for themselves
Thus they last forever

Therefore, the Son of God humbles Himself [b]
But finds Himself exalted
He sacrificed His life for everyone [c]
Yet, His Spirit remains alive in us
Through selfless action
This is how the Son of God achieves His purpose

[a] 1 John 2:16-17 *(for all that is in the world - the desire of the flesh, the desire of the eyes, the pride in riches - comes not from the Father but from the world. And the world and its desire are passing away, but those who do the will of God live forever.)*
Isaiah 65:17, Revelation 21:1

[b] Matthew 23:11-12 *(The greatest among you will be your servant. All who exalt themselves will be humbled, and all who humble themselves will be exalted.)*
Philippians 2:5-11

[c] John 17:1-5 *(After Jesus had spoken these words, he looked up to heaven and said, "Father, the hour has come; glorify your Son so that the Son may glorify you, since you have given him authority over all people, to give eternal life to all whom you have given him. And this is eternal life, that they may know you, the only true God, and Jesus Christ whom you have sent. I glorified you on earth by finishing the work that you gave me to do. So now, Father, glorify me in your own presence before the world existed.)*
John 14:16-17, John 14:26, John 15:12-13

Chapter 8
The Master Servant

The highest goodness is like water [a]
It nourishes all things without competing
It resides in low places people disdain [b]
Therefore, it is like God [c]

In dwelling, He remains in the right place [d]
In thinking, He loves with great depth [e]
In giving, He conveys great kindness
In words, He speaks truthfully [f]
In ruling, He leads with justice
In works, He is capable of miracles [g]
In action, He fulfills promises on time [h]

Thus, He does not trespass against others [i]
He is free from fault

[a] Isaiah 44:3 *(For I will pour water on the thirsty land, and streams on the dry ground; I will pour my spirit upon your descendants, and my blessing on your offspring.)*

[b] Luke 14:10 *(But when you are invited, go and sit down at the lowest place, so that when your host comes, he may say to you, "Friend, move up higher'; then you will be honored in the presence of all who sit at the table with you.)*

[c] John 14:11 *(Believe me that I am in the Father and the Father is in me; but if you do not, then believe me because of the works themselves.)*
John 1:1-2, 1 John 4:7-12

[d] John 1:14-18 *(And the Word became flesh and lived among us, and we have seen his glory, the glory as of a father's only son, full of grace and truth…)*

[e] 1 Timothy 1:12-14 *(I am grateful to Christ Jesus our Lord, who has strengthened me, because he judged me faithful and appointed me to his service, even though I was formerly a blasphemer, a persecutor, and a man of violence…)*
Galatians 5:22-23

[f] Psalm 9:7-8 *(But the Lord sits enthroned forever, he has established his throne for judgment. He judges the world with righteousness; he judges the peoples with equity.)*

[g] John 14:13 *(I will do whatever you ask whatever you ask in my name, so that the Father may be glorified in the Son.)*

[h] Luke 22:37 *(For I tell you, this scripture must be fulfilled in me, 'And he was counted among the lawless'; and indeed, what is written about me is being fulfilled.")*

[i] 1 John 3:4-6 *(Everyone who commits sin is guilty of lawlessness; sin is lawlessness. You know that he was revealed to take away sins, and in him there is no sin. No one who abides in him sins; no one who sins has either seen or known him.)*
1 Peter 2:22-25

Chapter 9
Being Excessive

Keep filling your stomach and you will vomit [a]
It is better to stop short

Keep sharpening your sword [b]
And the sword will break

Secure your life with the love of money [c]
And no one can protect it

Riches and titles bring arrogance [d]
And disaster will follow

When you achieve and acquire fame [e]
Remain humble
This is the Way of God

a Proverbs 23:1-8 *(...Do not eat the bread of the stingy; do not desire their delicacies; for like hair in the throat, so are they. "Eat and drink!" they say to you; but they do not mean it. You will vomit up the little you have eaten, and you will waste your pleasant words.)*

b Matthew 26:51-52 *(Suddenly one of those with Jesus put his hand on his sword, drew it, and struck the slave of the high priest, cutting off his ear. Then Jesus said to him, "Put your sword back into its place; for all who take the sword will perish by the sword.)*
Psalm 7:12-16

c 1 Timothy 6:6-10 *(Of course there is great gain in godliness combined with contentment; for we brought nothing into the world so that we can take nothing out of it; but if we have food and clothing, we will be content with these. But those who want to be rich fall into temptation and are trapped by many senseless and harmful desires that plunge people into ruin and destruction. For the love of money is a root of all kinds of evil, and in their eagerness to be rich some have wandered away from the faith and pierced themselves with many pains.)*

d Matthew 23:5-8 *(They do all their deeds to be seen by others; for they make their phylacteries broad and their fringes long. They love to have the place of honor at banquets and the best seats in the synagogues, and to be greeted with respect in the market places, and to have people call them rabbi. But you are not to be called rabbi, for you have one teacher and you are all students.)*
Habakkuk 2:5

e Matthew 23:12 *(All who exalt themselves will be humbled, and all humble themselves will be exalted.)*
Sirach 3:18-20

Chapter 10
The Spirit of God

To be filled by the Spirit of God and embrace Oneness [a]
Can you be still without temptation?

To quiet your soul and attain suppleness [b]
Can you be weaned like a child?

To be free of worldly views [c]
Can you take the plank out of your own eye?

To love all people and rule the country [d]
Can you be without cleverness?

To enter the opening and closing gate of Heaven [e]
Can you live according to the Word of God?

To understand the Word as taught by the Spirit [f]
Can you hold back your own words?
He created us [g]
He nurtures us

He gives life without possessing [h]
He achieves without taking credit [i]

He leads without dominating [j]
This is the mystic virtue of the Spirit [k]

[a] 1 Corinthians 6:17-20 (...Or do you not know that your body is a temple of the Holy Spirit within you, which you have from God, and that you are not your own?...)
Matthew 26:41, Psalm 46:10, John 17:20-24

[b] Psalm 131:1-2 (...But I have calmed and quieted my soul, like a weaned child with its mother; my soul is like the weaned child that is with me.)

[c] Matthew 7:4-5 (...You hypocrite, first take the log out of your own eye, and then you will see clearly to take the speck out of your neighbor's eye.)

[d] Matthew 23:1-7 (..."The scribes and the Pharisees sit on Moses' set; therefore, do whatever they teach you and follow it; but do not do as they do, for they do not practice what they teach...)

[e] John 1:1-2 (In the beginning was the Word, and the Word was with God, and the Word was God...)
1 John 2:5, Luke 11:28, Genesis 28:17

[f] 1 Corinthians 2:13-14 (And we speak of these things in words not taught by human wisdom but taught by the Spirit, interpreting spiritual things to those who are spiritual.)

[g] Genesis 1:24-27 (...So God created humankind in his image, in the image of God he created them; male and female he created them.)
1 Peter 1:23-25, John 4:10-14

[h] 2 Corinthians 6:10 (as sorrowful, yet always rejoicing; as poor, yet making many rich; as having nothing, yet possessing everything.)

[i] John 8:54 (Jesus answered, "If I glorify myself, my glory is nothing. It is my Father who glorifies me, he of whom you say, "He is our God,')
Hebrews 5:5

[j] Psalm 9:8 (He judges the world with righteousness; he judges the peoples with equity.)

[k] John 3:5-6 (What is born of the flesh is flesh, and what is born of the Spirit is spirit.)
Romans 5:15

Chapter 11
Body and Spirit

We assemble spokes to make a wheel
But the usefulness is the emptiness of the hole that allows rotation

We shape clay to make a pot [a]
But the usefulness is the emptiness that holds the water

We hammer wood together to make a house [b]
But the usefulness is the emptiness that provides the livable space

Therefore, what profit is the body [c]
Without the emptiness indwelt by the Holy Spirit?

[a] Isaiah 64:8 *(Yet, O Lord, you are our Father; we are the clay, and you are our potter, we are all the work of your hand.)*
Jeremiah 18:1-11

[b] 2 Timothy 3:16-17 *(All scripture is inspired by God and is useful for teaching, for reproof, for correction, and for training in righteousness, so that everyone who belongs to God may be proficient, equipped for every good work.)*
Habakkuk 2:14

[c] Romans 5:3-8 *(And not only that, but we also boast in our sufferings, knowing that suffering produces endurance, and endurance produces character, and character produces hope, and hope does not disappoint us, because God's love has been poured into our hearts through the Holy Spirit that has been given to us. For while we were still weak, at the right time Christ died for the ungodly. Indeed, rarely will anyone die for a righteous person - though perhaps for a good person someone might actually dare to die. But God proves his love for us in that while we still were sinners Christ died for us.)*
1 Corinthians 3:16

Chapter 12
Living in the Spirit

Sight betrays the eye [a]
Noise deafens the ear [b]

Gluttony dulls the taste [c]
Racing and wild hunting trouble the mind [d]
Worldly treasures confuse the heart [e]

Thus, the wise seek the Spirit and not the flesh [f]
Reject the external and choose the internal [g]

[a] John 9:41 *(Jesus said to them, "If you were blind you would not have sin. But now that you say "We see," your sin remains.)*

[b] Ecclesiastes 12:4 *(when the doors on the streets are shut, and the sound of the grindstone is low, and one rises at the sound of a bird, and all the daughters of song are brought low;)*
Mark 4:9, 1 Kings 19:12

[c] Romans 14:17 *(For the kingdom of God is not food and drink but righteousness and peace and joy in the Holy Spirit.)*
Proverbs 23:19-21, Colossians 2:16-19, Philippians 3:19

[d] Psalm 37:7-9 *(Be still before the Lord and wait patiently for him; do not fret over those who prosper in their way, over those who carry out evil devices. Refrain from anger and forsake wrath. Do not fret - it only leads to evil. For the wicked shall be cut off, but those who wait for the Lord shall inherit the land.)*
Proverbs 19:21

[e] Matthew 18:7 *(Woe to the world because of stumbling blocks! Occasions for stumbling are bound to come, but woe to the one by whom the stumbling block comes!)*
1 John 2:10, Romans 14:13

[f] John 6:63 *(It is the Spirit that gives life; the flesh is useless. The words that I have spoken to you are spirit and life.)*
Matthew 26:41, Philippians 3:3

[g] 1 Samuel 16:7 *(But the Lord said to Samuel, "Do not look on his appearance or the height of his stature, because I have rejected him; for the Lord does not see as mortals see; they look on the outward appearance, but the Lord looks on the heart.")*

Chapter 13
Great Misfortune

Honor and humility can be equally fearful [a]
Great misfortune is the ego
Why do we say, "Honor and humility can be equally fearful"?
Honor is high, humility is low
Gaining it makes one fearful
Losing it makes one fearful
That is why both honor and humility can be equally fearful

Why do we say, "Great misfortune is the ego"?
The reason I have suffering
Is that I am attached to the ego
If I am not attached to the ego
What misfortune will I have?

If you value the world as your own self [b]
You are fit to be trusted by the world
If you love the world as your own self
You are worthy to inherit the world

[a] Matthew 23:27-32 *("Woe to you, scribes and Pharisees, hypocrites! For you are like whitewashed tombs, which on the outside look beautiful, but inside they are full of bones of the dead and of all kinds of filth. So, you also on the outside look righteous to others, but inside you are full of hypocrisy and lawlessness. Woe to you, scribes and Pharisees, hypocrites. For you build the tombs of the prophets and decorate the graves of the righteous, and you say, 'If we had lived in the days of our ancestors, we would not have taken part with them in shedding the blood of the prophets Thus you testify against yourselves that you are descendants of those who murdered the prophets. Fill up, then, the measure of your ancestors.")*
Isaiah 13:11, Luke 14:11, James 4:6

[b] Deuteronomy 11:11-12 *(But the land that you are crossing over the occupy is a land of hills and valleys, watered by rain from the sky, a land that the Lord your God looks after. The eyes of the Lord are always on it, from the beginning of the year to the end of the year.)*
John 15:9-17, Luke 9:25, Numbers 35:33-34

Chapter 14
Presence of God

We look and do not see it [a]
And call it invisible
We listen and do not hear it [b]
And call it silent
We reach and do not grasp it [a]
And call it formless
These three cannot be fathomed [c]
Thus, they are joined into One

Above, there is no brightness [d]
Below, there is no darkness
Infinite, unnamable [e]
Returning to the realm of nothingness
The form of the formless
The image of the imageless
Indefinable, beyond all imagination [f]
Approach it, there is no beginning [a]
Follow it, there is no end

When one knows the Spirit of the ancient past [g]
One can begin to understand the present
Knowing the mystery of the beginning
Is the way to know God

[a] Romans 1:20-21 *(Ever since the creation of the world his eternal power and divine nature, invisible though they are, have been understood and seen through the things he has made. So they are without excuse; for though they knew God, they did not honor him as God or give thanks to him, but they became futile in their thinking, and their senseless minds were darkened.)*
John 14:17

[b] John 8:47 *(Whoever is from God hears the words of God. The reason you do not hear them is that you are not from God.)*
Mark 4:12

[c] Jude 20-21 *(But you, beloved, build yourselves up on your most holy faith; pray in the Holy Spirit; keep yourselves in the love of God; look forward to the mercy of our Lord Jesus Christ that leads to eternal life.)*
1 Corinthians 2:6-16

[d] Isaiah 60:19 *(The sun shall no longer be your light by day, nor for brightness shall the moon give light to you by night; but the Lord will be your everlasting light, and your God will be your glory.)*

[e] Colossians 1:15-16 *(He is the image of the invisible God, the first born of all creation; for in him all things in heaven and on earth were created, things visible and invisible, whether thrones or dominions or rulers or powers - all things have been created through him and for him.)*
Isaiah 40:28

[f] Job 9:10-11 *(who does great things beyond understanding, and marvelous things without number. Look, he passes by me, and I do not see him; he moves on, but I do not perceive him.)*

[g] John 1:1-2 *(In the beginning was the Word and the Word was with God, and the Word was God. He was in the beginning with God.)*
John 14:6-7, John 8:14-18

Chapter 15
Power in Stillness

The chosen are most profound and subtle [a]
Their wisdom is measureless
We cannot discover its depth
All we can do is describe their appearance

Careful, like men crossing thin ice [b]
Watchful, like men waiting for their master [c]
Courteous, like a guest [d]
Yielding, like melting ice [e]
Simple, like an uncarved block of wood [f]
Open-minded, like a widespread valley [g]
Non-revealing, like muddy water [h]

Who can be still while the muddy water clears?
It is in stillness that the mind becomes clear [i]
Who can be calm and yet persist?
It is in stillness that the right action arises

Men of God do not need to be self-fulfilled [j]
Since they have no desire to be self-fulfilled
They can live in the present moment

[a] Ecclesiastes 7:23-25 *(All this I have tested by wisdom; I said, "I will be wise," but it was far from me. That which is, is far off, and deep, very deep; who can find it out?...)*
1 Kings 4:29-34

[b] Ephesians 5:15-17 *(Be careful then how you live, not as unwise people but as wise, making the most of the time, because the days are evil...)*
Luke 21:34, 1 Corinthians 8:9

[c] Luke 12:35-40 *("Be dressed for action and have your lamps lit; be like those who are waiting for their master to return...)*

[d] Luke 14:10-11 *(But when you are invited, go and sit down at the lowest place, so that when your host comes, he may say to you, "Friend, move up higher'; then you will be honored...)*

[e] Psalm 1:1-3 *(...They are like trees planted by streams of water, which yield their fruit in its season, and their leaves do not wither. In all that they do, they prosper.)*

[f] 1 Corinthians 3:10-15 *(According to the grace of God given to me, like a skilled master builder I laid a foundation, and someone else is building on it...)*

[g] Isaiah 40:4 *(Every valley shall be lifted up, and every mountain and hill be made low; the uneven ground shall become level, and the rough places a plain.)*
Psalm 23:4, Matthew 7:7-8

[h] Numbers 5:16-31 *(...the priest shall take holy water in an earthen vessel, and take some of the dust that is on the floor of the tabernacle and put it into the water...)*
Proverbs 25:26, John 8:54, Matthew 7:6

[i] Psalm 46:10 *("Be still, and know that I am God! I am exalted among the nations, I am exalted in the earth.")*
Psalm 37:7-8, Luke 8:24-25

[j] 1 Thessalonians 2:13 *(We also constantly give thanks to God for this, that when you received the word of God that you heard from us, you accepted it not as a human word but as what it really is, God's word, which is also at work in you believers.)*
Galatians 5:16-18, James 4:13-17

Chapter 16
Restoration

Be clear-minded to attain emptiness [a]
Hold firm to the stillness
The rising and falling of all things will end [b]
I bear witness to their return [c]

All comes from dust, and to dust all shall return [d]
Returning is achieving perfect stillness [b]
Stillness is returning to the nature of God [b]
Returning to the nature of God is the Eternal [e]

Knowing the Eternal is insight [f]
Not knowing the never-changing leads to misfortune
Knowing the never-changing embraces all
Embracing all is impartiality
Impartiality is an attribute of sovereignty [g]
And sovereignty is of Heaven

He who is of Heaven is One with God [h]
He who is One with God is Eternal [e]
Count yourself dead but eternally alive in the Son of God [i]

[a] Zechariah 2:10-13 *(...The Lord will inherit Judah as his portion in the holy land, and will again choose Jerusalem. Be silent, all people, before the Lord; for he has roused himself from his holy dwelling.)*
Philippians 2:5-8

[b] 1 Peter 4:7 *(The end of all things is near; therefore be serious and discipline yourself for the sake of your prayers.)*
Revelation 21:1-8, Luke 2:34-35

[c] Ezra 1:3 *(Any of those among you who are of his people—may their God be with them!—are now permitted to go up to Jerusalem in Judah, and rebuild the house of the Lord, the God of Israel—he is the God who is in Jerusalem;)*
John 11:25, John 3:5-8,

[d] Ecclesiastes 3:20-21 *(All go to one place; all are from the dust, and all turn to dust again. Who knows whether the human spirit goes upward and the spirit of animals goes downward to the earth?)*

[e] John 1:1-2 *(In the beginning was the Word, and the Word was with God, and the Word was God. He was in the beginning with God.)*
John 13:1-3, John 12:23-25, John 6:40, 1 Peter 1:23,

[f] Romans 11:33-34 *(O the depth of the riches and wisdom and knowledge of God! How unsearchable are his judgments...)*
Revelation 2:7, Joel 2:28, Revelation 21:6-8

[g] 1 Peter 1:17 *(If you invoke as Father the one who judges all people impartially according to their deeds, live in reverent fear during the time of your exile.)*
1 Peter 4:8-11, Luke 6:35

[h] Revelation 5:6 *(Then I saw between the throne and the four living creatures and among the elders a Lamb standing as if it had been slaughtered, having seven horns and seven eyes, which are he seven spirits of God sent out into all the earth.)*
Revelation 19:1-3

[i] Romans 6:1-14 *(...The death he died, he died to sin, once for all; but the life he lives, he lives to God. So you also must consider yourselves dead to sin and alive to God in Christ Jesus...)*

Chapter 17
The Blind

When the King of Kings speaks [a]
The people do not know He is among them

The next best alternative is a recognized leader whom people
  praise and love [b]

The next is an intimidating leader whom people fear [c]

The worst is an incompetent leader whom people despise [d]
They have no faith
Have no faith in them

The Master proceeds calmly [a]

He fulfills His promise and settles matters [e]
Then the people say, "Amazing, we did it naturally!"

[a] John 10:25-39 *(Jesus answered, "I have told you, and you do not believe. The works that I do in my Father's name testify to me; but you do not believe, because you do not belong to my sheep...)*
John 1:10-14

[b] John 12:12-13 *(The next day the great crowd that had come to the festival heard that Jesus was coming to Jerusalem. So they took branches of palm trees and went out to meet him, shouting, "Hosanna! Blessed is the one who comes in the name of the Lord - the King of Israel!")*
John 8:54-56

[c] Matthew 23:1-8 *(Then Jesus said to the crowds and to his disciples, "The scribes and the Pharisees sit on Moses' seat; therefore, do whatever they teach you and follow it; but do not do as they do, for they do not practice what they teach...)*

[d] John 9:39-41 *(Jesus said, "I came into this world for judgment so that those who do not see may see, and those who do see may become blind." Some of the Pharisees near him heard this and said to him, "Surely we are not blind, are we?" Jesus said to them, "If you were blind, you would not have sin. But now that you say, 'We see,' your sin remains.)*

[e] John 19:28-30 *(After this, when Jesus knew that all was now finished, he said (in order to fulfill the scripture), "I am thirsty." A jar full of sour wine was standing here. So they put a sponge full of the wine on a branch of hyssop and held it to his mouth. When Jesus had received the wine, he said, "It is finished." Then he bowed his head and gave up his spirit.")*

Chapter 18
The Self

When people abandon God's Way
Their own self-righteousness appears [a]

When people turn to cleverness
Their own deception appears

When people lose harmony in the family [b]
Their emphasis on family values appears

When the people are confused and in chaos [c]
Their false minister appears

[a] Exodus 32:1-10 (...*The Lord said to Moses, "Go down at once! Your people, whom you brought out of the land of Egypt, have acted perversely; they have been quick to turn aside from the way that I commanded them; they have cast for themselves an image of a calf and have worshipped it and sacrificed to it, and said, 'These are your gods, O Israel, who brought you up out of the land of Egypt!'"...*)
1 Corinthians 3:18-21

[b] 1 Timothy 5:8 (*And whoever does not provide for relatives, and especially for family members, has denied the faith and is worse than an unbeliever.*)

[c] Jeremiah 23:16 (*Thus says the Lord of hosts: Do not listen to the words of the prophets who prophesy to you; they are deluding you. They speak visions of their own minds, not from the mouth of the Lord.*)

Chapter 19
Being Superficial

Do away with your display of sainthood, abandon cleverness [a]
So people can benefit a hundredfold

Do away with your display of kindness, abandon
    self-righteousness
So people can return to faithfulness and love

Do away with your display of cleverness, abandon profiteering
So bandits and thieves will no longer exist

These three things are superficial and not sufficient in themselves
Hence, know these higher principles: [b]

Show your true nature and embrace simplicity [c]
Diminish selfishness and reduce desire

[a] Matthew 23:27-28 *("Woe to you, scribes and Pharisees, hypocrites! For you are like whitewashed tombs, which on the outside look beautiful, but inside they are fill of the bones of the dead and of all kinds of filth. So you also on the outside look righteous to others, but inside you are full of hypocrisy and lawlessness.)*
James 3:13-18, 1 Corinthians 2:4-5, James 1:21, 1 Timothy 6:3-5

[b] 2 Timothy 3:16-17 *(All scripture is inspired by God and is useful for teaching, for reproof, for correction and for training in righteousness, so that everyone who belongs to God may be proficient, equipped for every good work.)*

[c] Philippians 2:3-8 *(Do nothing from selfish ambition or conceit, but in humility regard others as better than yourselves. Let each of you look not to your own interests, but to the interest of others. Let the same mind be in you that was in Christ Jesus, who though he was in the form of God, did not regard equality with God as something to be exploited, but emptied himself, taking the form of a slave, being born in human likeness. And being found in human form, he humbled himself and became obedient to the point of death - death on a cross.)*
Romans 8:5, Galatians 5:17, Mark 4:19

Chapter 20
Follower of God

Refrain from pointless learning
And your troubles will end [a]

What if people agree or disagree? [b]
What if people are good or bad?
Must you fear what others fear?
Such nonsense! How limitless!

Other people take enjoyment [c]
As if they are at a sacrificial feast
As if climbing up to the high terrace in spring

I alone am still and quiet [d]
Like a weaned child not yet smiling
So weary, drifting in the wind wherever it pleases [e]

The people have all they want [f]
I have nothing others possess
I alone am a fool for God
Ordinary people display intelligence
I alone appear muddled
Ordinary people are sharp and clever
I alone appear slow and dim

I drift along the waves of the sea [e]
Blown aimless in the wind without boundaries

Ordinary people are busy with goals rooted in this world [f]
I alone am stubborn and refuse the world
Indeed, I alone am different from the world
And favor nourishment from God above

[a] 1 Corinthians 8:1-13 *(Now concerning food sacrificed to idols: we know that "all of us possess knowledge." Knowledge puffs up, but love builds up. Anyone who claims to know something does not yet have the necessary knowledge, but anyone who loves God is known by him...)*
1 Corinthians 3:19, Proverbs 14:7-8

[b] Galatians 2:6 *(And from those who were supposed to be acknowledged leaders [what they actually were makes no difference to me; God shows no partiality] - those leaders contributed nothing to me.)*
Ecclesiastes 9:1-2, Ecclesiastes 12:13-14, Matthew 5:43-48

[c] 1 Corinthians 8:7-8 *(It is not everyone, however, who has this knowledge. Since some have become so accustomed to idols until now, they still think of the food they eat as food offered to an idol; and their conscience, being weak, is defiled...)*
Exodus 32:18-21

[d] Psalm 131:1-3 *(O Lord, my heart is not lifted up, my eyes are not raised too high; I do not occupy myself with things too great and too marvelous for me. But I have calmed and quieted my soul, like a weaned child with its mother; my soul is like the weaned child that is with me. O Israel, hope in the Lord from this time on and forevermore.)*

[e] Isaiah 48:18-19 *(O that you had paid attention to my commandments! Then your prosperity would have been like a river, and your success like the waves of the sea; your offspring would have been like the sand, and your descendants like its grains; their name would never be cut off or destroyed from before me.)*
Psalm 107:23-30, John 3:8

[f] John 15:18-19 *("If the world hates you, be aware that it hated me before it hated you. If you belonged to the world, the world would love you as its own. Because you do not belong to the world, but I have chosen you out of the world - therefore the world hates you.)*
1 John 2:15-17, 1 Corinthians 4:1-20

Chapter 21
Temple of the Spirit

The Spirit of great virtue
Follows the Word according to God alone [a]

The Word that became flesh [b]
Seems indefinable, seems unfathomable

So unfathomable, so indefinable
And yet within it there is form

So indefinable, so unfathomable
And yet within it there is substance

So deep, so profound
And yet within it there is Spirit [a]

The Spirit of God is supremely real
And yet within it there is faith

From the beginning to the present [c]
The Spirit has always been present
In order to proclaim the source of all things

How do I know the true nature of the source? [d]
By what lives within me

[a] John 14:26 *(But the Advocate, the Holy Spirit, whom the Father will send in my name, will teach you everything. And remind you of all that I have said to you.)*

Ephesians 3:14-18, Galatians 4:6

[b] John 1:1-18 (…And the Word became flesh and lived among us, and we have seen his glory, the glory as of a father's only son, full of grace and truth…)

Judith 16:2

[c] Matthew 28:18-20 *(And Jesus came and said to them, "All authority in heaven and on earth has been given to me. Go, therefore and make disciples of all nations, baptizing them in the name of the Father and of the Son and of the Holy Spirit, and teaching them to obey everything that I have commanded you. And remember, I am with you always, to the end of the age.")*

1 Corinthians 3:16-17

[d] Romans 8:9-11 *(But you are not in the flesh; you are in the Spirit, since the Spirit of God dwells in you. Anyone who does not have the Spirit of Christ does not belong to him. But if Christ is in you, though the body is dead because of sin, the Spirit is life because of righteousness. If the Spirit of him who raised Jesus from the dead dwells in you, he who raised Christ from the dead will give life to your mortal bodies also through his Spirit that dwells in you.)*

1 Corinthians 6:19

Chapter 22
Divine Wholeness

Remain yielding to become whole [a]
Remain bending to become straight
Remain empty to become filled

The weary will be renewed [b]
The poor will receive
The abundance will be confused

Therefore, the Master embraces Oneness [c]
To be an example for the world

Because He does not exalt himself [d]
He shines forth
Because He does not look to justify himself [e]
He becomes distinguished
Because He does not boast of himself [f]
He gains merit
Because He does not glorify himself
He endures
Because He does not contend [e]
He cannot be contended against

The ancients said, "Remain yielding to become whole"
Were they speaking empty words?

Become whole and you will return to harmony [a]

[a] Psalm 37:7-24 *(Be still before the Lord, and wait patiently for him; do not fret over those who prosper in their way, over those who carry out evil devices...)*
Luke 3:4-6, Hebrews 13:5, Matthew 11:28-30

[b] Isaiah 40:31 *(but those who wait for the Lord shall renew their strength, they shall mount up with wings like eagles, they shall run and not be weary, they shall walk and not faint.)*

[c] John 17:22-23 *(The glory that you have given me, I have given them, so that they may be one, as we are one. I in them and you in me, that they may become completely one, so that the world may know that you have sent me and have loved them even as you have loved me.)*
John 17:11

[d] Matthew 23:12 *(All who exalt themselves will be humbled, and all who humble themselves will be exalted.)*

[e] Luke 16:15 *(So he said to them, "You are those who justify yourselves in the sight of others; but God knows your hearts; for what is prized by human beings is an abomination in the sight of God.)*
Matthew 27:11-26

[f] John 17:1-9 *(...So now Father, glorify me in your own presence with the glory that I had in your presence before the world existed...)*
John 8:54-55

Chapter 23
You Reap What You Sow

Let your words be naturally short [a]
Strong wind does not last all morning
Sudden rain does not last all day

What causes this? Heaven and Earth! [b]
If Heaven and Earth do not cause violent things to last,
How much less should you?

Those who follow God are with God [c]
Those who follow the Spirit are with the Spirit
Those who follow transgression are with transgression

When you follow God, God is One with you
When you follow the Spirit, the Spirit is One with you
When you follow transgression, transgression is One with you

For whatever your faith lacks, faith cannot provide [d]

[a] Proverbs 10:19 *(When words are many, transgression is not lacking, but the prudent are restrained in speech.)*
Proverbs 17:27-28

[b] Genesis 1:1-2 *(In the beginning when God created the heavens and the earth, the earth was a formless void and darkness covered the face of the deep, while a wind from God swept over the face of the waters.)*

[c] Galatians 6:7-10 *(Do not be deceived; God is not mocked, for you reap whatever you sow. If you sow to your own flesh, you will reap corruption from the flesh; but if you sow to the Spirit, you will reap eternal life from the Spirit...)*
Galatians 5:22-26

[d] Mark 4:39-41 *(He woke up and rebuked the wind, and said to the sea, "Peace! Be still!" Then the wind ceased and there was a dead calm. He said to them, "Why are you afraid?" Have you still no faith?" And they were filled with great awe and said to one another, "Who then is this, that even the wind and the sea obey him?")*
Matthew 14:27-31

Chapter 24
The Ego

Those who tiptoe above others cannot stand firm [a]

Those who are not still before God will not walk far [b]

Those who glorify themselves will not shine [c]

Those who vaunt their self-righteousness will not be distinguished [d]

Those who praise themselves will have no merit

Those who boast about themselves will not last

Followers of God call such things leftover food and unnecessary
They are despised by everyone

Thus, those who live in the Spirit of God do not rely on them [e]

[a] Proverbs 16:18 *(Pride goes before destruction, and a haughty spirit before a fall.)*
1 Peter 5:5-6, Matthew 18:6-9

[b] Psalm 37:7 *(Be still before the Lord, and wait patiently for him; do not fret over those who prosper in their way, over those who carry out evil devices.)*

[c] Matthew 23:12 *(All who exalt themselves will be humbled, and all who humble themselves will be exalted.)*

[d] 1 Corinthians 1:24-31 *(but to those who are called, both Jews and Greeks, Christ the power of God and the wisdom of God. For God's foolishness is wiser than human wisdom, and God's weakness is stronger than human strength…)*
Matthew 23:25

[e] Galatians 5:16-17 *(Live by the Spirit, I say, and do not gratify the desires of the flesh. For what the flesh desires is opposed to the Spirit, and what the Spirit desires is opposed to the flesh; for these are opposed to each other, to prevent you from doing what you want.)*

Chapter 25
The Great

There is something formless and eternal [a]
Before the Heavens and Earth were created

So silent! So unfathomable!
Independent and unchanging
Omnipresent and inexhaustible
Maker of the Heavens and Earth

I do not know His name [b]
For lack of a name, I call Him God
Forced to name God further; I call Him "Great"

Being Great, God flows through all things [c]
Flowing everywhere, far and deep
Reaching far and deep, He returns

Hence, God is Great [a]
He makes the Heavens Great
He makes the Earth Great
He makes the Master Great
The four Greats in the universe
Thus the Master is one of the Great

Man follows the natural laws of Earth [d]
Earth follows the natural laws of the Heavens
The Heavens follow the natural laws of God
God follows the laws of His own nature

[a] Genesis 1:1-31 *(In the beginning when God created the heavens and the earth, the earth was a formless void and the darkness covered the face of the deep, while a wind from God swept over the face of the waters...)* Colossians 1:15-20

[b] Exodus 3:13-14 *(But Moses said to God, "If I come to the Israelites and say to them, 'The God of your ancestors has sent me to you,' and they ask me, 'What is his name?' what shall I say to them?" God said to Moses, "I AM WHO I AM." He said further, "Thus you shall say to the Israelites, "I AM has sent me to you.")*

[c] Psalm 139:7-10 *(Where can I go from your spirit? Or where can I flee from your presence? If I ascend to heaven, you are there; if I make my bed in Sheol, you are there. If I take the wings of the morning and settle at the farthest limits of the sea, even there your hand shall lead me, and your right hand shall hold me fast.)*

[d] Romans 1:18-21 *(For the wrath of God is revealed from heaven against all ungodliness and wickedness of those who by their wickedness suppress the truth. For what can be known about God is plain to them, because God has shown it to them. Ever since the creation of the world his eternal power and divine nature, invisible though they are, have been understood and seen through the things he has made. So they are without excuse; for though they knew God, they did not honor him as God or give thanks to him, but they became futile in their thinking, and their senseless minds were darkened.)*

Chapter 26
Foundation of the Son of God

The heavy foundation of the Son of God is the root of lightness [a]

Stillness is the master of restlessness [b]

The Son of God travels all day without losing sight of His purpose [c]
Not tempted by sights of splendor
He remains unshaken and transcends beyond
How unfortunate would it be if the Son of God were lightly swayed?

If you let yourself be lightly blown away [a]
You separate from your roots

If you let restlessness move you [b]
You separate from the Spirit

[a] Matthew 7:24-29 *("Everyone who hears these words of mine and acts on them will be like a wise man who built his house on rock. The rain fell, the floods came, and the winds blew and beat on that house, but it did not fall, because it had been founded on rock. And everyone who hears these words of mine and does not act on them will be like a foolish man who built his house on sand. The rain fell, and the floods came and the winds blew and beat against that house and it fell - and great was its fall!" Now when Jesus had finished saying these things, the crowds were astounded at his teaching, for he taught them as one having authority, and not as their scribes.)*

[b] Psalm 37:7 *(Be still before the Lord, and wait patiently for him; do not fret over those who prosper in their way, over those who carry out evil devices.)*

[c] Matthew 4:1-11 *(Then Jesus was led up by the Spirit into the wilderness to be tempted by the devil. He fasted forty days and forty nights, and afterwards he was famished. The tempter came and said to him, "If you are the Son of God, command these stones to become loaves of bread." But he answered, "It is written, 'One does not live by bread alone but by every word that comes from the mouth of God.'" Then the devil took him to the holy city and placed him on the pinnacle of the temple…)*

Chapter 27
Essential Wonder of God

Good travelers do not leave tracks [a]
Good orators do not seek errors [b]
Good reckoners do not use counters [c]

Good rulers need no bars [d]
Thus no one can open it
Good binders need no ropes
Thus no one can untie it

Therefore, God saves others [e]
And abandons no one
God saves all things
And abandons nothing
This is called following the light of God

Therefore, good men are teachers of bad men [f]
Bad men are lessons for good men
If you fail to value and learn the lessons from your teachers
Then intelligence counts for nothing

This is the essential wonder of God's love [g]

[a] Mark 6:8-9 *(He ordered them to take nothing for their journey except a staff; no bread, no bag, no money in their belts; but to wear sandals and not to put on two tunics.)*

[b] Luke 6:37 *("Do not judge and you will not be judged; do not condemn and you will not be condemned. Forgive, and you will be forgiven;)*

[c] Matthew 18:21-22 *(Then Peter came and said to him, "Lord, if another member of the church sins against me, how often should I forgive? As many as seven times?" Jesus said to him, "Not seven times, but, I tell you, seventy-seven times.)*
1 Corinthians 13:4-6

[d] Mark 1:22 *(They were astounded at his teaching, for he taught them as one having authority, and not as the scribes.)*

[e] 1 Peter 3:18 *(For Christ also suffered for sins once for all, the righteous for the unrighteous, in order to bring you to God. He was put to death in the flesh, but made alive in the spirit,)*

[f] Matthew 5:17-20 *("Do not think that I have come to abolish the law or the prophets; I have come not to abolish but to fulfill. For truly I tell you, until heaven and earth pass away, not one letter, not one stroke of a letter will pass from the law until all is accomplished. Therefore, whoever breaks one of the least of these commandments, and teaches others to do the same, will be called least in the kingdom of heaven; but whoever does them and teaches them will be called great in the kingdom of heaven. For I tell you, unless your righteousness exceeds that of the scribes and Pharisees, you will never enter the kingdom of heaven.)*

[g] Ephesians 2:4-10 *(But God, who is rich in mercy, out of the great love with which he loved us even when we were dead through our trespasses, made us alive together with Christ - by grace you have been saved - and raised us up with him and seated us with him in the heavenly places in Christ Jesus, so that in ages to come he might show the immeasurable riches of his grace in kindness toward us in Christ Jesus. For by grace you have been saved through faith, and this is not your own doing; it is the gift of God - not the result of works, so that no one may boast. For we are what he has made us, created in Christ Jesus for good works, which God prepared beforehand to be our way of life.)*

Chapter 28
Simplicity

Know the nature of the masculine
But hold to the feminine [a]

Be the stream of living water [b]
Being the stream of living water
The Eternal Spirit will not depart
Returning you to a weaned child

Know the source of light within
But hold to the dark [c]

Be a good example to the world [d]
Being a good example to the world
The Eternal Spirit will not deviate
Returning you to a limitless nature

Know the virtue of honor
Yet hold to humility [e]
Be satisfied taking the lowest place
Being satisfied with the lowest place
The Eternal Spirit shall be sufficient
Retuning you to the natural state of simplicity

Tools are shaped by the Master Carpenter from a block of plain
     wood to become useful [f]

The wise make use of them and then become leaders [g]
Thus, remain undivided by keeping to the simplicity of the block

[a] Genesis 1:27 *(So God created humankind in his image; in the image of God he created them; male and female he created them.)*
Numbers 5:5-7

[b] John 7:37-39 *(On the last day of the festival, the great day, while Jesus was standing there, he cried out, "Let anyone who is thirsty come to me, and let the one who believes in me drink. As the scripture has said, 'Out of the believer's heart shall flow rivers of living water.'" Now he said this about the Spirit, which believers in him were to receive; for as yet there was no Spirit, because Jesus was not yet glorified.)*
John 4:10

[c] 2 Corinthians 4:4-6 *(In their case the god of this world has blinded the minds of the unbelievers, to keep them from seeing the light of the gospel of the glory of Christ, who is the image of God...)*

[d] Titus 2:1-15 *(But as for you, teach what is consistent with sound doctrine. Tell the older men to be temperate, serious, prudent, and sound in faith, in love, and in endurance...)*

[e] Luke 14:7-11 *(When he noticed how the guests chose the places of honor, he told them a parable. "When you are invited by someone to a wedding banquet, do not sit down at the place of honor, in case someone more distinguished than you has been invited by your host; and the host who invited both of you may come and say to you, 'Give this person your place,' and then in disgrace you would start to take the lowest place...)*

[f] Ecclesiastes 12:11-12 *(The sayings of the wise are like goads, and like nails firmly fixed are the collected sayings that are given by one shepherd. Of anything beyond these, my child, beware. Of making many books there is no end, and much study is a weariness of the flesh.)*
Proverbs 30:5-6, Revelation 22:18

[g] Deuteronomy 5:1 *(Moses convened all Israel, and said to them: Hear, O Israel, the statutes and ordinances that I am addressing to you today; you shall learn them and observe them diligently.)*

Chapter 29
Better Left Alone

Can you better the world? [a]
I know that it cannot done
The world is a sacred vessel
You can neither control nor improve it
If you try to change it, you will fail
If you hold on to it, you will lose it

In fact, consider the things of nature: [a]
Some things either lead or follow
Some things either breathe fast or slow
Some things either have strength or weakness
Some things either remain standing or are taken down

Therefore, the wise avoid extremes, excess, and extravagance [b]

[a] Ecclesiastes 3:1-22 *(For everything there is a season, and a time for every matter under heaven; a time to be born, and time to die; a time to plant, and a time to pluck up what is planted; a time to kill, and a time to heal; a time to break down, and a time to build up; a time to weep, and a time to laugh; a time to mourn and a time to dance; a time to throw away stones, and a time to gather stones together; a time to embrace, and a time to refrain from embracing; a time to seek, and a time to lose; a time to keep, and a time to throw away; a time to tear, and a time to sew; a time to keep silence, and a time to speak; a time to love, and a time to hate; a time for war, and a time for peace. What gain have the workers from their toil? I have seen the business that God has given to everyone to be busy with. He has made everything suitable for its time; moreover he has put a sense of past and future into their minds, yet they cannot find out what God has done from the beginning to the end...)*

Job 38:1-41

[b] Ecclesiastes 7:15-18 *(In my vain life I have seen everything; there are righteous people who perish in their righteousness, and there are wicked people who prolong their life in their evil-doing. Do not be too righteous, and do not act too wise; why should you destroy yourself? Do not be too wicked, and do not be a fool; why should you die before your time? It is good that you should take hold of the one, without letting go of the other; for the one who fears God shall succeed in both.)*

Chapter 30
The Fulfillment

Those who rely on God to advise the ruler
Maintain control of the world without weapons
For all who draw the sword will die by the sword [a]

Wherever army troops camp
Thistles and thorns grow [b]
In the wake of a great war follow years of famine

The Master fulfills His purpose, then stops [c]
And does not take advantage of His power to reach domination [a]

He fulfills His purpose but does not boast [d]
He fulfills His purpose but does not take glory
He fulfills His purpose but is not arrogant
He fulfills His purpose but only by necessary means [c]
He fulfills His purpose but without force [a]

Strong forces become powerful for a period of time but they will
    come to an end [e]
This is contrary to the everlasting God
That which is contrary to God soon ends

[a] Matthew 26:50-56 (*…Suddenly, one of those with Jesus put his hand on his sword, drew it, and struck the slave of the high priest, cutting off his ear. Then Jesus said to him, "Put your sword back into its place; for all who take the sword will perish by the sword…*)

[b] Matthew 24:4-8 (*Jesus answered them, "Beware that no one leads you astray. For many will come in my name, saying, 'I am the Messiah!' and they will lead many astray. And you will hear of wars and rumors of wars; see that you are not alarmed; for this must take place, but the end is not yet. For nation will rise against nation, and kingdom against kingdom, and there will be famines and earthquakes in various places: all this is but the beginning of the birth pangs.*)

[c] John 19:28-30 (*After this, when Jesus knew that all was now finished, he said (in order to fulfill the scripture), "I am thirsty." A jar full of sour wine was standing there. So they put a sponge full of the wine on a branch of hyssop and held it to his mouth. When Jesus had received the wine, he said, "It is finished." Then he bowed his head and gave up his spirit.*)

[d] Ephesians 2:8-10 (*For by grace you have been saved through faith, and this is not your own doing; it is the gift of God—not the result of works, so that no one may boast. For we are what he has made us, created in Christ Jesus for good works, which God prepared beforehand to be our way of life..*)
Hebrews 5:5, John 8:54

[e] Revelation 21:6-10 (*Then he said to me, "It is done! I am the Alpha and the Omega, the beginning and the end. To the thirsty I will give water as a gift from the spring of the water of life. Those who conquer will inherit these things, and I will be their God and they will be my children. But as for the cowardly, the faithless, the polluted, the murderers, the fornicators, the sorcerers, the idolaters, and all liars, their place will be in the lake that burns with fire and sulfur, which is the second death."…*)
Revelation 22:12-15

Chapter 31

Weapons of the World

Weapons are the tools of misfortune [a]
All wise men detest them
Those who live by the Spirit of God avoid weapons of the world
Men of peace value the left side
Men of war value the right side

Weapons of the world are tools of misfortune
They are not tools of righteous men
When using it out of necessity [b]
Stillness and quietude are above all
And victory is no occasion for rejoicing [c]

Those who do not guard their lips in victory [d]
Pride themselves in killing
And those who pride themselves in killing
Will never find fulfillment in the world

Joyful occasions are given to the left
And sad occasions are given to the right
The lieutenant general stands on the left
And the commander-in-chief stands on the right

Thus, the result of war is conducted like a funeral [e]
The multitude of people who have been killed
Should be mourned with tears
This is why the victory of war is observed as a funeral

[a] 2 Corinthians 10:2-6 *(I ask that when I am present I need not show boldness by daring to oppose those who think we are acting according to human standards. Indeed, we live as human beings, but we do not wage war according to human standards; for the weapons of our warfare are not merely human, but they have divine power to destroy strongholds. We destroy arguments and every proud obstacle raised up against the knowledge of God, and we take every thought captive to obey Christ. We are ready to punish every disobedience when your obedience is complete.)* Matthew 26:52-54, Ecclesiastes 9:16-18, Proverbs 13:14

[b] Psalm 37:7-9 *(Be still before the Lord, and wait patiently for him; do not fret over those who prosper in their way, over those who carry out evil devices. Refrain from anger, and forsake wrath. Do not fret - it leads only to evil. For the wicked shall be cut off, but those who wait for the Lord shall inherit the land.)*

[c] Proverbs 24:17-18 *(Do not rejoice when your enemies fall, and do not let your heart be glad when they stumble, or else the Lord will see it and be displeased, and turn away his anger from them.)*

[d] Proverbs 21:30-31 *(No wisdom, no understanding, no counsel, can avail against the Lord. The horse is made ready for the day of battle, but the victory belongs to the Lord.)* Proverbs 13:1-21

[e] Romans 12:19 *(Beloved, never avenge yourselves, but leave room for the wrath of God; for it is written, "Vengeance is mine, I will repay; says the Lord.")* Matthew 5:22

Chapter 32
Sovereign God

God is eternally nameless [a]
Simple and subtle [b]
No one can take hold of Him

If powerful leaders can hold on to God [c]
All will worship Him on their own
The Heavens and Earth will be harmonious [d]
Good fortune will rain from above
People will naturally live in peace without using force

In the beginning of creation the primal simplicity differentiated
    with names [e]
Different names begin to increase with complexity
One must know when to stop
Knowing when to stop prevents danger

Everything is born of God and will return to Him [f]
Like the rivers of the land flowing into the ocean [g]

[a] Exodus 3:13-15 *(But Moses said to God, "If I come to the Israelites and say to them, 'The God of your ancestors has sent me to you,' and they ask me, 'What is his name?' what shall I say to them?" God said to Moses, "I AM WHO I AM." He said further, "Thus you shall say to the Israelites, 'I AM has sent me to you.'" God also said...)*

[b] Colossians 1:15-17 *(He is the image of the invisible God, the first both of all creation; for in him all things in heaven and on earth were created, things visible and invisible, whether thrones or dominions or rulers or powers - all things have been created through him and for him. He himself is before all things, and in him all things hold together.)*

[c] Daniel 4:1-3 *(King Nebuchadnezzar to all peoples, nations, and languages that live throughout the earth: May you have abundant prosperity! The signs and wonders that the Most High God has worked for me I am pleased to recount...)*
John 4:21-24

[d] Revelation 21:1-5 *(Then I saw a new heaven and a new earth; for the first heaven and the first earth had passed away, and the sea was no more. And I saw the holy city, the new Jerusalem, coming down out of heaven from God, prepared as a bride adorned for her husband. And I heard a loud voice from the throne saying, "See, the home of God is among mortals. He will dwell with them; they will be his peoples, and God himself will be with them; he will wipe every tear from their eyes...)*
Isaiah 11:6-9, Revelation 2:7

[e] Genesis 2:19-20 *(So out of the ground the Lord God formed every animal of the field and every bird of the air, and brought them to the man to see what he would call them; and whatever the man called every living creature, that was its name...)*

[f] Ecclesiastes 3:20 *(All go to one place; all are from the dust, and all turn to dust again.)*
Ecclesiastes 12:7

[g] Ecclesiastes 1:7 *(All streams run to the sea, but the sea is not full; to the place where the streams flow, there they continue to flow.)*

Chapter 33
Self-Awareness

Knowing others is knowledge [a]
But knowing yourself is true wisdom

Mastering others is strength [b]
But mastering yourself is true power

To be content, you are truly rich [c]
To be faithful, you have willpower [d]

To be deeply rooted, you will endure [e]
To die but not perish, is to live eternally [f]

[a] 2 Corinthians 13:5 *(Examine yourselves to see whether you are living in the faith. Test yourselves. Do you not realize that Christ Jesus is in you? - unless, indeed, you fail to meet the test!)*
Proverbs 24:3-7; Proverbs 2:6

[b] 1 Corinthians 4:1-14 *(...But with me it is a very small thing that I should be judged by you or by any human court. I do not even judge myself. I am not aware of anything against myself, but I am not thereby acquitted. It is the Lord who judges me...)*

[c] Philippians 4:11-13 *(Not that I am referring to being in need; for I have learned to be content with whatever I have. I know what it is to have little, and I know what it is to have plenty. In any and all circumstances I have learned the secret of being well-fed and of going hungry, of having plenty and of being in need. I can do all things through him who strengthens me.)*

[d] Hebrews 11:24-31 *(By faith, Moses, when he was grown up, refused to be called a son of Pharaoh's daughter, choosing rather to share ill-treatment with the people of God than to enjoy the fleeting pleasures of sin. He considered abuse suffered for the Christ to be far greater wealth than the treasures of Egypt, for he was looking ahead to the reward...)*

[e] Matthew 13:18-23 *(...But as for what was sown on good soil, this is the one who hears the word and understands it, who indeed bears fruit and yields, in one case a hundredfold, in another sixty, and in another thirty.")*
Matthew 13:37-39

[f] 1 Peter 1:23 *(You have been born anew, not of perishable but of imperishable seed, through the living and enduring word of God.)*
Romans 7:4-13

Chapter 34
Living Water

The Spirit of God is like a river of living water [a]
It flows to every corner of the world

All things depend on it for life [b]
And it never stops

It fulfills its purpose without taking glory [c]
It clothes and feeds new life to many, but does not control [a]

Ever desiring nothing of this world [d]
It seems insignificant
All things return to it but it does not control [e]
It can be named "Great" [f]

Even in the end, it does not declare itself as Great [g]
Thus, it achieves Greatness

[a] John 7:37-39 *(On the last day of the festival, the great day, while Jesus was standing there, he cried out, "Let anyone who is thirsty come to me, and let the one who believes in me drink. As the scripture has said, 'Out of the believer's heart shall flow rivers of living water.'" Now he said this about the Spirit, which believers in him were to receive; for as yet there was no Spirit, because Jesus was not yet glorified.)*

[b] John 15:1-8 *("I am the true vine, and my Father is the vinegrower. He removes every branch in me that bears no fruit. Every branch that bears fruit he prunes to make it bear more fruit...)*

[c] John 8:50-54 *(Yet I do not seek my own glory; there is one who seeks it and he is the judge. Very truly, I tell you, whoever keeps my word will never see death."...)*
Philippians 2:5-8

[d] Matthew 19:21 *(Jesus said to him, "If you wish to be perfect, go, sell your possessions, and give the money to the poor, and you will have treasure in heaven, then come, follow me.")*

[e] Ecclesiastes 3:20-21 *(All go to one place; all are from the dust, and all turn to dust again. Who knows whether the human spirit goes upward and the spirit of animals goes downward to the earth?)*
Ecclesiastes 1:7

[f] Luke 1:32 *(He will be great, and will be called the Son of the Most High, and the Lord God will give to him the throne of his ancestor David.)*

[g] Hebrews 12:1-2 *(Therefore, since we are surrounded by so great a cloud of witnesses, let us also lay aside every weight and the sin that clings so closely, and let us run with perseverance the race that is set before us, looking to Jesus the pioneer and perfecter of our faith, who for the sake of the joy that was set before him endured the cross, disregarding its shame, and has taken his seat at the right hand of the throne of God.)*
Hebrews 1:1-6

Chapter 35
Mystical Word of God

Receive the Spirit of God [a]
For the world will come together as One

Those who come will receive no harm [b]
But will find peace and joy

The sound of music and good food [c]
Make travelers stop for momentary pleasure
But the spoken Word of God
Sounds plain without a taste for life

When you look for it, it is hidden [d]
When you listen to it, it is silent
Yet when used, it is beyond measure

[a] 1 Corinthians 12:12-31 *(For just as the body is one and has many members, and all the members of the body, though many, are one body, so it is with Christ. For in the one Spirit we were all baptized into one body - Jews or Greeks, slave or free - and we were all made to drink of the one Spirit…)*

[b] 1 John 5:18 *(We know that those who are born of God do not sin, but the one who was born of God protects them, and the evil one does not touch them.)*

[c] Exodus 32:1-21 *(…They rose early the next day, and offered burnt offerings and brought sacrifices of well-being; and the people sat down to eat and drink, and rose up to revel. The Lord said to Moses, "Go down at once! Your people, whom you brought up out of the land of Egypt, have acted perversely; they have been quick to turn aside from the way that I commanded them; they have cast for themselves an image of a calf, and have worshiped it and sacrificed to it, and said, 'These are your gods, O Israel, who brought you up out of the land of Egypt!'"…)*

[d] Mark 4:21-25 *(He said to them, "Is a lamp brought in to be put under the bushel basket, or under the bed, and not on the lampstand? For there is nothing hidden, except to be disclosed; nor is anything secret, except to come to light. Let anyone with ears to hear listen!" And he said to them, "Pay attention to what you hear; the measure you give will be the measure you get, and still more will be given you. For to those who have, more will be given; and from those who have nothing, even what they have will be taken away.")*
Matthew 13:10-17

Chapter 36
Natural Order

What is shrunken [a]
Must have first been expanded
What is weakened
Must have first been strengthened

What is cast down [b]
Must have first been exalted

What is received [c]
Must have first been given
This is the subtle perception of things [d]

The gentle and yielding overcome the hard and forceful [e]
Just as fish cannot leave deep waters [d]
So too the inner workings of the Heavenly kingdom
Cannot be revealed to the people

[a] 1 Peter 1:24-25 *(For "All flesh is like grass and all its glory like the flower of grass. The grass withers, and the flower falls, but the word of the Lord endures forever." That word is the good news that was announced to you.)*
Galatians 6:1-3

[b] Luke 14:7-11 *(...But when you are invited, go and sit down at the lowest place, so that when your host comes, he may say to you, 'Friend, move up higher'; then you will be honored in the presence of all who sit at the table with you. For all who exalt themselves will be humbled, and those who humble themselves will be exalted.")*
Matthew 27:27-31

[c] Luke 12:48 *(But the one who did not know and did what deserved a beating will receive a light beating. From everyone to whom much has been given, much will be required; and from the one to whom much has been entrusted, even more will be demanded.)*
Acts 20:35

[d] Matthew 11:25-27 *(At that time Jesus said, "I thank you, Father, Lord of heaven and earth, because you have hidden these things from the wise and intelligent and have revealed them to infants; yes, Father, for such was your gracious will. All things have been handed over to me by my Father; and no one knows the Son except the Father, and no one knows the Father except the Son and anyone to whom the Son chooses to reveal him.)*

[e] 2 Corinthians 12:10 *(Therefore I am content with weaknesses, insults, hardships, persecutions, and calamities for the sake of Christ; for whenever I am weak, then I am strong.)*
1 Corinthians 1:27

Chapter 37
Absence of Desire

The unchanging God is in non-action [a]
Yet through Him all things are done

If powerful leaders live according to God [b]
The world will transform itself
Even if people begin to desire
They will be drawn back by the simplicity of God

The simplicity of God
Brings absence of desire
The absence of desire leads to stillness
Thus, the world will be One in harmony [c]

[a] Ecclesiastes 3:9-15 *(What gain have the workers from their toil? I have seen the business that God has given to everyone to be busy with. He had made everything suitable for its time; moreover he has put a sense of past and future into their minds, yet they cannot find out what God has done from the beginning to the end. I know that there is nothing better for them than to be happy and enjoy themselves as long as they live; moreover, it is God's gift that all should eat and drink and take pleasure in all their toil. I know that whatever God does endures forever; nothing can be added to it, nor anything taken from it; God has done this, so that all should stand in awe before him. That which is, already has been; that which is to be, already is; and God seeks out what has gone by.)*
James 1:17, Daniel 7:14

[b] 2 Peter 1:3-8 *(His divine power has given us everything needed for life and godliness, through the knowledge of him who called us by his own glory and goodness. Thus he has given us, through these things, his precious and very great promises, so that through them you may escape from the corruption that is in the world because of lust, and may become participants of the divine nature. For this very reason, you must make every effort to support your faith with goodness, and goodness with knowledge, and knowledge with self-control, and self-control with endurance, and endurance with godliness, and godliness with mutual affection, and mutual affection with love. For if these things are yours and are increasing among you, they keep you from being ineffective and unfruitful in the knowledge of our Lord Jesus Christ.)*
Romans 8:5-6, Romans 12:2, John 16:12-16

[c] 1 Corinthians 1:10 *(Now I appeal to you, brothers and sisters, by the name of our Lord Jesus Christ, that all of you be in agreement and that there be no divisions among you, but that you be united in the same mind and the same purpose.)*
John 17:23, Romans 12:16

Chapter 38
The Seed of God

Truly good people do not proclaim their goodness [a]
And are therefore truly good
Foolish people speak of their goodness [b]
And are therefore truly not good

Truly good people remain still according to the Spirit [a]
And act with no agenda
Foolish people take action according to the flesh [b]
And act with agenda

Kind people act regardless of merit [c]
And act without agenda
Self-righteous people act to gain merit [d]
And act with agenda

Highly ritual people act to gain merit [e]
And when people do not respond
They pull up their sleeves and enforce order

Therefore, when the Way of God is lost, goodness appears [f]
When goodness is lost, kindness appears
When kindness is lost, self-righteousness appears
When self-righteousness is lost, ritual appears

Ritual is the shell of faith and truth [f]
And the beginning of chaos
As to foreknowledge, it is our own flowery knowledge of God
And the beginning of folly

Therefore a truly great man dwells in the depths of God and [g]
    not the surface
He seeks the seed of the fruit and not the flower
Truly, he prefers what is within and discards the outer

[a] 1 Thessalonians 2:3-7 *(For our appeal does not spring from deceit or impure motives or trickery, but just as we have been approved by God to be entrusted with the message of the gospel, even so we speak, not to please mortals, but to please God who tests our hearts...)*

[b] Colossians 2:18-19 *(Do not let anyone disqualify you, insisting on self-abasement and worship of angels, dwelling on visions, puffed up without cause by a human way of thinking, and not holding fast to the head, from whom the whole body, nourished and held together by its ligaments and sinews, grows with a growth that is from God.)*

[c] Leviticus 19:18 *(You shall not take vengeance or bear a grudge against any of your people, but you shall love your neighbor as yourself: I am the Lord.)*

[d] Matthew 23:1-4 *(Then Jesus said to the crowds and to his disciples, "The scribes and the Pharisees sit on Moses' seat; therefore do whatever they teach you and follow it; but do not do as they do, for they do not practice what they teach. They tie up heavy burdens, hard to bear, and lay them on the shoulders of others; but they themselves are unwilling to lift a finger to move them.)*

[e] Matthew 23:5-7 *(They do all their deeds to be seen by others; for they make their phylacteries broad and their fringes long. They love to have the place of honor at banquets and the best seats in the synagogues, and to be greeted with respect in the market places, and to have people call them rabbi.)*

[f] Matthew 23:23-27 *("Woe to you, scribes and Pharisees, hypocrites! For you tithe mint, dill, and cumin, and have neglected the weightier matters of the law; justice and mercy and faith...)*

[g] Luke 6:45 *(The good person out of the good treasure of the heart produces good, and the evil person out of evil treasure produces evil; for it is out of the abundance of the heart that the mouth speaks.)*
Romans 15:1

Chapter 39
Humility

In the beginning, the Heavens and Earth attained Oneness [a]
The sky attained Oneness and became clear
The Earth attained Oneness and became still
The Spirit attained Oneness and became divine
The valley attained Oneness and became abundant
The myriad of things attained Oneness and became alive
The rulers attained Oneness and became sovereign
These all arise from the Oneness of God

Without clarity, the sky will break open with hailstones [b]
Without stillness, the Earth will tremble and quake
Without divinity, the Spirit will vanish
Without abundance, the valley will dry up
Without life, the myriad of things will be extinct
Without sovereignty, the rulers will fall

Humility is the root of honor [c]
The high is built upon the foundation of the low
Thus, true rulers call themselves alone and unworthy
Don't they depend on being humble and low? Absolutely!
Therefore, seeking praise does not win true praise
Do not adorn yourself with sparkling jade [d]
But be common and dull as the rocks

[a] Exodus 3:13-15 *(But Moses said to God, "If I come to the Israelites and say to them, 'The god of your ancestors has sent me to you,' and they ask me, 'What is his name?' what shall I say to them?" God said to Moses, "I AM WHO I AM." He said further, "Thus you shall say to the Israelites, 'I AM has sent me to you.'" God also said to Moses, "Thus you shall say to the Israelites, 'The Lord the God of your ancestors, the God of Abraham, the God of Isaac, the God of Jacob, has sent me to you': This is my name forever, and this is my title for all generations.)*
Psalm 102:25-27, Genesis 1:31, Ecclesiastes 3:9-15

[b] Mark 13:5-8 *(Then Jesus began to say to them, "Beware that no one leads you astray. Many will come in my name and say 'I am he!' and they will lead many astray. When you hear of wars and rumors of wars, do not be alarmed; this must take place, but the end is still to come. For nation will rise against nation, and kingdom against kingdom; there will be earthquakes in various places; there will be famines. This is but the beginning of the birth pangs.)*
Ezekiel 13:1-19

[c] Luke 14:10-11 *(But when you are invited, go and sit down at the lowest place, so that when your host comes, he may say to you, 'Friend, move up higher'; then you will be honored in the presence of all who sit at the table with you. For all who exalt themselves will be humbled, and those who humble themselves will be exalted.")*

[d] Matthew 23:5-7 *(They do all their deeds to be seen by others; for they make their phylacteries broad and their fringes long. They love to have the place of honor at banquets and the best seats in the synagogues, and to be greeted with respect in the marketplaces, and to have people call them rabbi.)*
Matthew 23:27

Chapter 40
Cycle of Life

The movement of God is returning [a]

The Way of God is yielding [b]

All things of the world are born of being [c]

Being arises from non-being [d]

[a] Ecclesiastes 3:18-20 *(I said in my heart with regard to human beings that God is testing them to show that they are but animals. For the fate of humans and the fate of animals is the same; as one dies, so dies the other. They all have the same breath, and humans have no advantage over the animals; for all is vanity. All go to one place; all are from the dust, and all turn to dust again.)*

[b] Psalm 37:4-7 *(Take delight in the Lord, and he will give you the desires of your heart. Commit your way to the Lord; trust in him, and he will act. He will make your vindication shine like the light, and the justice of your cause like the noonday. Be still before the Lord, and wait patiently for him; do not fret over those who prosper in their way, over those who carry out evil devices.)*
Exodus 32:14, Jonah 3:9-10

[c] Genesis 2:7 *(then the Lord God formed man from the dust of the ground, and breathed into his nostrils the breath of life; and the man became a living being.)*
Genesis 1:30

[d] Colossians 1:15-16 *(He is the image of the invisible God, the firstborn of all creation, for in him all things in heaven and on earth were created, things visible and invisible, whether thrones or dominions or rulers or powers - all things have been created through him and for him.)*

Chapter 41
Mysterious Nature of God

When the wise hear the Word of God
They obey faithfully [a]
When ordinary people hear the Word of God
They believe for a while but sometimes doubt it
When foolish people hear the Word of God
They laugh out loud [b]
If foolish people did not laugh
It would not be the Word of God

Thus, as it was written in ancient times:
The bright path appears dark [c]
The advancement of God appears to retreat [d]
The straight path appears crooked [e]
The highest virtue appears empty [f]
The utmost purity appears tainted [g]
The promised Word appears hopeless [h]
The greatest virtue appears weak [i]
The divine truth appears untrue [j]
The perfect square appears shapeless [k]
The finest talent appears unproductive [l]
The voice of God appears silent [m]

The nameless God has no form [n]
Invisible, hidden in our hearts
He alone nourishes and brings everything to completion

[a] Mark 4:18-20 (…*And these are the ones sown on the good soil: they hear the word and accept it and bear fruit, thirty and sixty and a hundredfold.*")
2 Peter 1:10-11

[b] Job 12:4 (*I am a laughingstock to my friends; I, who called upon God and he answered me, a just and blameless man, I am a laughingstock.*)
Isaiah 30:12

[c] John 3:19 (*And this is the judgment, that the light has come into the world, and people loved darkness rather than light because their deeds were evil.*)
1 John 2:8-9

[d] Matthew 20:17-19 (…"*See, we are going up to Jerusalem, and the Son of Man will be handed over to the chief priests and scribes, and they will condemn him to death;…*)

[e] John 21:18-19 (…*you will stretch out your hands, and someone else will fasten a belt around you and take you where you do not wish to go.*" … *After this he said to him, "Follow me.*")

[f] Matthew 16:21 (*From that time on, Jesus began to show his disciples that he must go to Jerusalem and undergo great suffering at the hands of the elders and chief priests and scribes, and be killed, and on the third day be raised.*)

[g] Luke 6:2-9 (…*The scribes and the Pharisees were watching Him closely to see if He healed on the Sabbath, so that they might find reason to accuse Him...*)

[h] 2 Peter 3:9 (*The Lord is not slow about his promise, as some think of slowness, but is patient with you, not wanting any to perish, but all to come to repentance.*)

[i] John 19:9-10 (…"*Where are you from?*" *But Jesus gave him no answer. Pilate therefore said to him, "Do you refuse to speak to me? Do you not know that I have power to release you, and power to crucify you?*")

[j] 2 Peter 3: 15-16 (…*There are some things in them hard to understand, which the ignorant and unstable twist to their own destruction, as they do the other scriptures.*)
John 18:36-37

[k] Luke 8:10 (…"*To you it has been given to know the secrets of the kingdom of God; but to others I speak in parables, so that 'looking they may not perceive, and listening they may not understand.'*)

[l] John 19:28-30 (*After this, when Jesus knew that all was now finished, he said (in order to fulfil the scriptures), "I am thirsty." A jar full of sour wine was standing there. So they put a sponge full of the wine on a branch of hyssop and held it to his mouth. When Jesus had received the wine, he said, "It is finished." Then he bowed his head and gave up his spirit.*)

[m] Matthew 27:46 (*And about three o'clock Jesus cried with a loud voice, "Eli, Eli, lema sabachthani?" that is, "My God, my God, why have you forsaken me?*")
Matthew 13:15-17

[n] Colossians 1:15-16 (*He is the image of the invisible God, the firstborn of all creation; for in him all things in heaven and on earth were created, things visible and invisible...*)
Revelation 21:6

Chapter 42
Harmony in Unity

God gives birth to One [a]
One gives birth to Two [b]
Two gives birth to Three [c]
Three gives birth to the myriad of things

The myriad of things in the world carries darkness [d]
And embraces the light of the Spirit
The two forces achieve harmony by remaining as One [e]

The people hate to be "helpless," "small," and "worthless" [f]
Yet these are the very names that wise rulers call themselves

Truly, one gains by losing [g]
Or one loses by gaining

I will teach what the wise rulers teach
For all who draw the sword will die by the sword [h]
This is a principle of my teaching

[a] Genesis 2:22 *(And the rib that the Lord God had taken from the man he made into a woman and brought her to the man.)*

[b] Genesis 1:27 *(So God created humankind in his image, in the image of God he created them; male and female he created them.)*

[c] Genesis 4:1 *(Now the man knew his wife Eve, and she conceived and bore Cain, saying, "I have produced a man with the help of the Lord.")*

[d] 2 Corinthians 4:6 *(For it is God who said, "Let light shine out of darkness," who has shone in our hearts to give the light of the knowledge of the glory of God in the face of Jesus Christ.)*
John 3:21, Ephesians 5:8

[e] Ephesians 5:31-32 *("For this reason a man will leave his father and mother and be joined to his wife, and the two will become one flesh." This is a great mystery, and I am applying it to Christ and the church.)*

[f] 1 Samuel 15:17 *(Samuel said, "Though you are little in your own eyes, are you not the head of the tribes of Israel? The Lord anointed you king over Israel.)*

[g] John 12:25 *(Those who love their life in this world will lose it, and those who hate their life in this world will keep it for eternal life.)*

[h] Matthew 26:52 *(Then Jesus said to him, "Put your sword back into its place; for all who take the sword will perish by the sword.)*

Chapter 43
Emanation of God

The softest things of the world [a]
Overcome the hardest things of the world

The formless Spirit which has no substance [b]
Enters the body which has no opening
That is how I know the advantage of non-interfering action [c]

The silent teaching without words [c]
The benefits of actions without interfering
This is the unmatched Way understood by few [d]

[a] 1 Corinthians 1:27-29 *(But God chose what is foolish in the world to shame the wise; God chose what is weak in the world to shame the strong; God chose what is low and despised in the world, things that are not, to reduce to nothing things that are, so that no one might boast in the presence of God.)*
2 Corinthians 12:10, Psalm 114:8

[b] 1 Corinthians 6:19-20 *(Or do you not know that your body is a temple of the Holy Spirit within you, which you have from God, and that you are not your own? For you were bought with a price; therefore glorify God in your body.)*

[c] Exodus 14:14 *(The Lord will fight for you, and you have only to keep still.)*
Psalm 37:7

[d] Mark 4:11-12 *(And he said to them, "To you has been given the secret of the kingdom of God, but for those outside, everything comes in parables; in order that 'they may indeed look, but not perceive, and may indeed listen, but not understand; so that they may not turn again and be forgiven.'")*

Chapter 44
Spiritual Wealth

Fame or the self: Which is dearer? [a]
The self or wealth: Which is more valuable? [b]
Gain or loss: Which is more painful?

Thus excessive love for things
Will cost you dearly at the end

Do not store up for yourselves treasures on Earth [c]
Where thieves break in and steal

Godliness with contentment
Avoids the disgrace of foolish desires

Knowing when to stop avoids trouble [d]
Thus, one can endure eternally [e]

[a] Matthew 23:1-12 *(…The greatest among you will be your servant. All who exalt themselves will be humbled, and all who humble themselves will be exalted.)*

[b] James 5:1-3 *(Come now, you rich people, weep and wail for the miseries that are coming to you. Your riches have rotted, and your clothes are moth-eaten. Your gold and silver have rusted, and their rust will be evidence against you, and it will eat your flesh like fire. You have laid up treasure for the last days.)*
1 Timothy 6:6-10, Proverbs 13:7

[c] Matthew 6:19-21 *(Do not store up for yourselves treasures on earth, where moth and rust consume and where thieves break in and steal; but store up for yourselves treasures in heaven, where neither moth nor rust consumes and where thieves do not break in and steal. For where your treasure is, there your heart will be also.)*

[d] Proverbs 13:8 *(Wealth is a ransom for a person's life, but the poor get no threats.)*

[e] James 2:5 *(Listen, my beloved brothers and sisters. Has not God chosen the poor in the world to be rich in faith and to be heirs of the kingdom that he has promised to those who love him?)*
Luke 18:22

Chapter 45
Path to Greatness

Great perfection seems imperfect [a]
But its lasting usefulness is unfailing

Great fullness seems empty [b]
And yet it is inexhaustible

Great straightness seems crooked [c]
Great skill seems clumsy [d]
Great eloquence seems silent [e]

Bustling-about overcomes cool times [f]
Stillness overcomes heated times
Thus, stillness and silence are the Way of nature

[a] Hebrews 12:2 *(…looking to Jesus the pioneer and perfecter of our faith, who for the sake of the joy that was set before him endured the cross, disregarding its shame, and has taken his seat at the right hand of the throne of God.)*
John 3:34, John 19:28-30

[b] Romans 11:33 *(O the depth of the riches and wisdom and knowledge of God! How unsearchable are his judgments and how inscrutable his ways!)*
1 Peter 1:18, John 1:16

[c] Luke 3:4-6 *(…'Prepare the way of the Lord, make his paths straight. Every valley shall be filled, and every mountain and hill shall be made low, and the crooked shall be made straight, and the rough ways made smooth; and all flesh shall see the salvation of God.' ")*

[d] 1 Samuel 17:41-50 *(…But David said to the Philistine, "You come to me with sword and spear and javelin; but I come to you in the name of the Lord of hosts, the God of the armies of Israel, whom you have defied. This very day the Lord will deliver you into my hand…)*

[e] Exodus 4:10-12 *(But Moses said to the Lord, "O my Lord, I have never been eloquent, neither in the past nor even now that you have spoken to your servant; but I am slow of speech and slow of tongue." Then the Lord said to him, "Who gives speech to mortals? Who makes them mute or deaf, seeing or blind? Is it not I, the Lord? Now go, and I will be with your mouth and teach you what you are to speak.")*

[f] Proverbs 29:11 *(A fool gives full vent to anger, but the wise quietly holds back.)*
Psalm 37:7-9, Matthew 27:12-14

Chapter 46
Contentment

When the world is right with God [a]
Horses retire to haul fertilizer on the fields

When the world is separate from God [b]
Horses trample the fields equipped for cavalry

There is no sin greater than excessive desire [c]
There is no disaster greater than discontentment
There is no misfortune greater than excessive greed

Thus, to know contentment is everlasting fulfillment [d]

[a] Romans 8:5-8 *(For those who live according to the flesh set their minds on the things of the flesh, but those who live according to the Spirit set their minds on the things of the Spirit. To set the mind on the flesh is death, but to set the mind on the Spirit is life and peace. For this reason the mind that is set on the flesh is hostile to God; it does not submit to God's law - indeed it cannot, and those who are in the flesh cannot please God.)*

[b] Jeremiah 6:8 *(Take warning, O Jerusalem, or I shall turn from you in disgust, and make you a desolation, an uninhabited land.)*
Isaiah 59:2

[c] 1 Timothy 6:6-10 *(Of course, there is great gain in godliness combined with contentment; for we brought nothing into the world, so that we can take nothing out of it; but if we have food and clothing, we will be content with these. But those who want to be rich fall into temptation and are trapped by many senseless and harmful desires that plunge people into ruin and destruction. For the love of money is a root of all kinds of evil, and in their eagerness to be rich some have wandered away from the faith and pierced themselves with many pains.)*
Ecclesiastes 5:10

[d] Philippians 4:11-13 *(Not that I am referring to being in need; for I have learned to be content with whatever I have. I know what it is to have little, and I know what it is to have plenty. In any and all circumstances I have learned the secret of being well-fed and of going hungry, of having plenty and of being in need. I can do all things through him who strengthens me.)*

Chapter 47
Inner Wisdom

Without going out of your door [a]
Seek within to know the world

Without looking out of your window
Have faith within to see the Way of God

The more you outwardly seek this world
The less you will know yourself

This is why the wise [b]
Know the world without going places

See the Way of God without looking [c]
And achieve without doing

[a] 2 Corinthians 4:16-18 *(So we do not lose heart. Even though our outer nature is wasting away, our inner nature is being renewed day by day. For this slight momentary affliction is preparing us for an eternal weight of glory beyond all measure, because we look not at what can be seen but at what cannot be seen; for what can be seen is temporary, but what cannot be seen is eternal.)*
John 20:29, Proverbs 17:24, 1 Samuel 16:7

[b] Colossians 3:16 *(Let the word of Christ dwell in you richly; teach and admonish one another in all wisdom; and with gratitude in your hearts sing psalms, hymns, and spiritual songs to God.)*
James 3:17

[c] Exodus 14:14 *(The Lord will fight for you, and you have only to keep still.")*
Psalm 37:7-9

Chapter 48
Be Still and Let God

Pursue knowledge, daily accumulation [a]
Pursue God, daily removal [b]

Less and less is done [c]
Until one reaches the state of stillness

By remaining still, anything is possible
To achieve in this world, one must let go [b]

Do not interfere [d]
The one who interferes cannot achieve in this world

[a] 1 Timothy 6:20-21 *(Timothy, guard what has been entrusted to you. Avoid the profane chatter and contradictions of what is falsely called knowledge; by professing it some have missed the mark as regards the faith. Grace be with you.)*
1 Corinthians 3:18-20, 1 Corinthians 13:8-12

[b] John 8:36 *(So if the Son makes you free, you will be free indeed.)*
2 Corinthians 5:17

[c] Psalm 37:7 *(Be still before the Lord, and wait patiently for him; do not fret over those who prosper in their way, over those who carry out evil devices.)*
Psalm 46:10, Exodus 14:14, John 19:28

[d] 1 Thessalonians 4:10-12 *(...But we urge you, beloved to do so more and more, to aspire to live quietly, to mind your own affairs, and to work with your hands, as we directed you, so that you might behave properly towards outsiders and be dependent on no one.)*
Proverbs 26:17

Chapter 49
The Good Shepherd

The Son of God does not have a mind of His own [a]
He embraces the mind of others as His own

He is righteous to the righteous [b]
He is righteous to the unrighteous
Thus, the virtue of righteousness

He is faithful to the faithful [c]
He is faithful to the unfaithful
Thus, the virtue of faithfulness

He lives in peace with everyone [d]
And merges His mind with the minds of the people [a]

The people follow Him with their eyes and ears [e]
He loves them all as His children [f]

[a] Romans 15:1-5 *(We who are strong ought to put up with the failings of the weak, and not to please ourselves. Each of us must please our neighbor for the good purpose of building up the neighbor. For Christ did not please himself; but as it is written, "The insults of those who insult you have fallen on me." For whatever was written in former days was written for our instruction, so that by steadfastness and by the encouragement of the scriptures we might have hope...)*
Philippians 2:1-8

[b] Matthew 5:43-48 *("You have heard that It was said, 'You shall love your neighbor and hate your enemy.' But I say to you, Love your enemies and pray for those who persecute you, so that you may be children of your father in heaven; for he makes his sun rise on the evil and on the good, and sends rain on the righteous and on the unrighteous...)*

[c] 2 Timothy 2:13 *(If we are faithless, he remains faithful - for he cannot deny himself.)*

[d] Acts 10:36 *(You know the message he sent to the people of Israel, preaching peace by Jesus Christ - he is Lord of all.)*
Romans 5:1

[e] John 10:14-18 *(I am the good shepherd. I know my own and my own know me, just as the Father knows me and I know the Father. And I lay down my life for the sheep. I have other sheep that do not belong to this fold. I must bring them also and they will listen to my voice. So there will be one flock, one shepherd...)*

[f] 1 John 5:1-2 *(Everyone who believes that Jesus is the Christ has been born of God, and everyone who loves the parent loves the child. By this we know that we love the children of God, when we love God and obey his commandments.)*
1 Peter 3:18

Chapter 50

To Die Is Gain

From birth to death [a]

Three in ten are followers of life

Three in ten are followers of death [b]

Three in ten live life and quickly step into death [c]

Why is this so?

Because they strive excessively for worldly life [d]

I heard whoever loses his life will find it [a]

When traveling the roads they encounter no rhinos or tigers [e]

When going into battle they are not harmed by weapons

Rhinos have nowhere to drive their horns

Tigers have nowhere to thrust their claws

Soldiers have nowhere to lodge their blades

Why is this so?

Because death no longer has mastery over them

[a] Matthew 10:39 *(Those who find their life will lose it, and those who lose their life for my sake will find it.)*

[b] Galatians 6:7-10 *(Do not be deceived; God is not mocked, for you reap whatever you sow. If you sow to your own flesh, you will reap corruption from the flesh; but if you sow to the Spirit, you will reap eternal life from the Spirit. So let us not grow weary in doing what is right, for we will reap at harvest time, if we do not give up; So then, whenever we have an opportunity, let us work for the good of all, and especially for those of the family of faith.)*

[c] Luke 8:13-14 *(The ones on the rock are those who, when they hear the word, receive it with joy. But these have no root; they believe for a while and in a time of testing fall away. As for what fell among the thorns, these are the ones who hear; but as they go on their way, they are choked by the cares and riches and pleasures of life, and their fruit does not mature.)*

[d] 1 John 2:15-17 *(Do not love the world or the things in the world. The love of the Father is not in those who love the world; for all that is in the world - the desire of the flesh, the desire of the eyes, the pride in riches - comes not from the Father but from the world. And the world and its desires are passing away, but* those who do the will of God live forever.)
Romans 12:2

[e] John 5:24-26 *(Very truly, I tell you, anyone who hears my word and believes him who sent me has eternal life, and does not come under judgment, but has passed from death to life. Very truly, I tell you, the hour is coming, and is now here, when the dead will hear the voice of the Son of God, and those who hear will live. For just as the Father has life in himself, so he has granted the Son also to have life in himself;)*
Romans 6:1-10, Revelation 2:10-11

Chapter 51

Mysterious Power of the Spirit

God creates all living things
Spirit nurtures them [a]
Matter shapes them [b]
Nature completes them [c]
Therefore, all things honor God and value the Spirit [d]
The honor to God, the value of Spirit
Is not by force but is spontaneously natural

Thus God created them [b]
Spirit nurtures them, grows them, protects them,
comforts them, educates them, shelters them [e]
Creates without possessing them [f]
Acts without taking credit [g]
Nurtures without dominating [a]
This is the mysterious power of the Spirit [h]

a Romans 8:26-27 *(Likewise the Spirit helps us in our weakness; for we do not know how to pray as we ought, but that very Spirit intercedes with sighs too deep for words. And God, who searches the heart, knows what is the mind of the Spirit, because the Spirit intercedes for the saints according to the will of God.)*

b Revelation 4:11 *("You are worthy, our Lord and God, to receive glory and honor and power, for you created all things, and by your will they existed and were created.")*
Genesis 2:7, Genesis 28:14

c Genesis 1:26 *(Then God said, "Let us make humankind in our image, according to our likeness; and let them have dominion over the fish of the sea, and over the birds of the air, and over the cattle, and over all the wild animals of the earth, and over every creeping thing that creeps upon the earth.")*

d 1 John 3:24 *(All who obey his commandments abide in him, and he abides in them. And by this we know that he abides in us, by the Spirit that he has given us.)*
 1 John 4:7-12

e Romans 8:26-27 *(Likewise the Spirit helps us in our weakness; for we do not know how to pray as we ought, but that very Spirit intercedes with sighs too deep for words. And God, who searches the heart, knows what is the mind of the Spirit, because the Spirit intercedes for the saints according to the will of God.)*
1 Corinthians 12:1-7, James 2:26

f 2 Corinthians 3:17 *(Now the Lord is the Spirit, and where the Spirit of the Lord is, there is freedom.)*
Galatians 5:13, Romans 8:2, Galatians 5:1

g Luke 6:32-36 *("If you love those who love you, what credit is that to you? For even sinners love those who love them. If you do good to those who do good to you, what credit is that to you? For even sinners do the same...)*

h 1 Corinthians 2:7-11 *(But we speak God's wisdom, secret and hidden, which God decreed before the ages for our glory. None of the rulers of this age understood this; for if they had, they would not have crucified the Lord of glory...)*

Chapter 52
Faith

The world begins with God [a]
The Creator of all things [b]

If you know the Eternal God [c]
You would know the Son
Anyone who has seen the Son
Has also seen the Eternal God whom we glorify
And at the end, there is no danger to fear [d]

Keep still and guard your mouth [e]
If you want to be fruitful

Keep active and speak of evil [e]
If you want to live without salvation

Seeing the truth is clarity [f]
Remaining in weakness is strength [g]

Receive the light of the Son [h]
And you will return to clarity
And be saved from harm [i]
This is called the practice of faith

[a] Genesis 1:1-2 *(In the beginning when God created the heavens and the earth, the earth was a formless void and darkness covered the face of the deep, while a wind from God swept over the face of the waters)*

[b] Colossians 1:15-16 *(He is the image of the invisible God, the firstborn of all creation; for in him all things in heaven and on earth were created, things visible and invisible…)*

[c] John 14:5-17 *(…"Lord, we do not know where you are going. How can we know the way?" Jesus said to him, "I am the way, and the truth, and the life. No one comes to the Father except through me…)*

[d] 2 Timothy 4:6-8 *(As for me, I am already being poured out as a libation, and the time of my departure has come. I have fought the good fight, I have finished the race, I have kept the faith…)*
John 14:27

[e] Proverbs 21:23 *(To watch over mouth and tongue is to keep out of trouble.)*
Luke 6:45, John 7:18

[f] John 3:16-21 *(…But those who do what is true come to the light, so that it may be clearly seen that their deeds have been done in God.")*

[g] 2 Corinthians 12:9-10 *(…but he said to me, "My grace is sufficient for you, for power is made perfect in weakness." So, I will boast all the more gladly of my weaknesses, so that the power of Christ may dwell in me.)*
1 Corinthians 1:27-31

[h] John 1:7-14 *(He came as a witness to testify to the light, so that all might believe through him. He himself was not the light, but he came to testify to the light…)*
John 4:24

[i] 1 Thessalonians 5:9-10 *(For God has destined us not for wrath but for obtaining salvation through our Lord Jesus Christ, who died for us, so that whether we are awake or asleep we may live with him.)*
John 3:36, Romans 2:8

Chapter 53
The Lost Way

If I have a bit of wisdom [a]
I can walk the path of God
And only fear to stray from it

God makes the Way straight and easy [b]
Yet people prefer to swerve to the right and left [c]

When the courts are arrayed in splendor [d]
The fields are full of weeds
And the granaries are empty

Some wear beautiful clothes [e]
And carry sharp swords
They overindulge in food and drink
And possess wealth they cannot use
They are a brood of vipers and hypocrites [f]
This is not the Way of God

[a] Proverbs 3:13-35 *(Happy are those who find wisdom and those who get understanding, for her income is better than silver, and her revenue better than gold. She is more precious than jewels and nothing you desire can compare with her…)*

Luke 17:6, Matthew 14:31

[b] Matthew 11:28-30 *("Come to me, all you that are weary and are carrying heavy burdens, and I will give you rest. Take my yoke upon you and learn from me; for I am gentle and humble in heart, and you will find rest for your souls. For my yoke is easy, and my burden is light.")*

[c] Proverbs 4:25-27 *(Let your eyes look directly forward, and your gaze be straight before you. Keep straight the path of your feet, and all your ways will be sure. Do not swerve to the right or to the left; turn your foot away from evil.)*

[d] Isaiah 10:1-2 *(Ah, you who make iniquitous decrees, who write oppressive statues, to turn aside the needy from justice and to rob the poor of my people of their right, that widows may be your spoil, and that you may make the orphans your prey!)*

Proverbs 22:7, Proverbs 28:15

[e] Matthew 23:25-28 *("Woe to you, scribes and Pharisees, hypocrites! For you clean the outside of the cup and of the plate, but inside they are full of greed and self-indulgence. You blind Pharisee! First clean the inside of the cup, so that the outside also may become clean. "Woe to you, scribes and Pharisees, hypocrites! For you are like whitewashed tombs, which on the outside look beautiful, but inside they are full of the bones of the dead and of all kinds of filth. So you also on the outside look righteous to others, but inside you are full of hypocrisy and lawlessness.)*

[f] Matthew 23:33 *(You snakes, you brood of vipers! How can you escape being sentenced to hell?)*

Chapter 54
Sowing Your Seed

Whoever sows the Word in good soil
Will not be uprooted [a]
Whoever faithfully embraces the Word
Will not slip away
Our descendants will honor the ancestral sacrifice for eternity

Sow the Word in yourself [b]
And it will be a genuine part of you
Sow the Word in your family
And it will be abundant
Sow the Word in your community
And it will be everlasting
Sow the Word in your country
And it will be prosperous
Sow the Word in the world
And it will be widespread

Therefore, recognize others as yourself [c]
Recognize families as your family
Recognize communities as your community
Recognize countries as your country
Recognize the world as the world

How do I know the world for what it is?
By what I sow in me [b]

[a] Luke 8:11-15 *("Now the parable is this: The seed is the word of God. The ones on the path are those who have heard; then the devil comes and takes away the word from their hearts, so that they may not believe and be saved. The ones on the rock are those who, when they hear the word, receive it with joy. But these have no root; they believe only for a while and in a time of testing fall away. As for what fell among the thorns, these are the ones who hear; but as they go on their way, they are choked by the cares and riches and pleasures of life, and their fruit does not mature. But as for that in the good soil, these are the ones who, when they hear the word, hold it fast in an honest and good heart, and bear fruit with patient endurance.)* Proverbs 10:30, Galatians 6:7-10

[b] Colossians 3:16 *(Let the word of Christ dwell in you richly; teach and admonish one another in all wisdom; and with gratitude in your hearts sing psalms, hymns, and spiritual songs to God.)* John 8:31

[c] Matthew 7:12 *("In everything do to others as you would have them do to you; for this is the law and the prophets.)*

Chapter 55

Perfect in Weakness

Those who are filled with the Spirit
Are like newborn infants [a]

Venomous serpents are no danger [b]
Wild beasts are no threat
Birds of prey do not attack
Their bones appear fragile and muscles weak [c]
But their grips are firm

They are unconcerned about sexual unity [d]
Yet, they are made complete and full of strength [e]

Their shouts are heard from afar without their voices
    getting hoarse [f]
That is because they are in harmony with the Spirit

Knowing harmony is to know that which is unchanging
Knowing that which is unchanging is to have wisdom [g]

Lusting after a greater life with excessive force invites misfortune [h]
To overuse the mind is to overload it
Things that are forced can grow strong for a while but soon
    fade away
This is not in harmony with God
And that which is not in harmony with God comes to an early end

[a] 1 Peter 2:2-3 *(Like newborn infants, long for the pure, spiritual milk, so that by it you may grow into salvation - if indeed you have tasted that the Lord is good.)*
Luke 1:15, 41

[b] 1 Peter 3:13-17 *(Now who will harm you if you are eager to do what is good? But even if you do suffer for doing what is right, you are blessed. Do not fear what they fear, and do not be intimidated, but in your hearts sanctify Christ as Lord…)*

[c] 2 Corinthians 12:9-10 *(but he said to me, "My grace is sufficient for you, for power is made perfect in weakness." So, I will boast all the more gladly of my weaknesses, so that the power of Christ may dwell in me...)*

[d] 1 Corinthians 7:8-9 *(To the unmarried and the widows I say that it is well for them to remain unmarried as I am. But if they are not practicing self-control, they should marry. For it is better to marry than to be aflame with passion.)*

[e] 1 John 4:16-18 *(So we have known and believe the love that God has for us. God is love, and those who abide in love abide in God, and God abides in them...)*

[f] Romans 8:26-27 *(Likewise the Spirit helps us in our weakness; for we do not know how to pray as we ought, but that very Spirit intercedes with sighs too deep for words. And God, who searches the heart, knows what is the mind of the Spirit, because the Spirit intercedes for the saints according to the will of God.)*

[g] Proverbs 9:10 *(The fear of the Lord is the beginning of wisdom, and the knowledge of the Holy One is insight.)*

[h] Psalm 37:7-15 *(Be still before the Lord, and wait patiently for him; do not fret over those who prosper in their way, over those who carry out evil devices. Refrain from anger, and forsake wrath. Do not fret - it only leads to evil…)*
Psalm 37:34-40, 1 John 2:17

Chapter 56
Oneness of God

Those who know do not talk [a]
Those who talk do not know

Close the mouth
Shut the door to senseless ideas [b]
Blunt the cunning ways
Unravel the daily entanglements [c]
Soften the glare of glory [d]
Become One with the dust of the world [e]
This is the mystic Oneness of God

Those who achieve the mystic Oneness of God
Are not affected by closeness [f]
Nor affected by abandonment
Are not affected by profiting
Nor affected by harming
Are not affected by honor
Nor affected by disgrace
Thus, the mystic Oneness of God is treasured by the world [g]

[a] 1 Samuel 2:3 *(Talk no more so very proudly, let not arrogance come from your mouth; for the Lord is a God of knowledge, and by him actions are weighed.)*
James 1:26, Proverbs 10:19

[b] Psalm 7:12-16 *(If one does not repent, God will whet his sword; he has bent and stung his bow; he has prepared his deadly weapons, making his arrows fiery shafts…)*
Matthew 23:1-12

[c] Romans 12:2 *(Do not be conformed to this world, but be transformed by the renewing of your minds, so that you may discern what is the will of God - what is good and acceptable and perfect.)*
Philippians 4:8-9, 1 Peter 5:7, Psalm 55:22

[d] Romans 3:22-24 *(the righteousness of God through faith in Jesus Christ for all who believe. For there is no distinction, since all have sinned and fall short of the glory of God; they are now justified by his grace as a gift, through the redemption that is in Christ Jesus,)*
John 8:54, 1 Corinthians 1:27

[e] John 17:20-24 *(…The glory that you have given me I have given them, so that they may be one, as we are one, I in them and you in me, that they may become completely one, so that the world may know that you have sent me and have loved them even as you have loved me…)*
Psalm 103:13-18, 1 Corinthians 12:12-14

[f] 2 Corinthians 6:3-13 *(We are putting no obstacle in anyone's way, so that no fault may be found with our ministry, but as servants of God we have commended ourselves in every way: through great endurance, in afflictions, hardships, calamities, beatings, imprisonments, riots, labors, sleepless nights, hunger; by purity, knowledge, patience, kindness, holiness of spirit, genuine love,…)*

[g] Ephesians 3:1-6 *(…In former generations this mystery was not made known to humankind, as it has now been revealed to his holy apostles and prophets by the Spirit:…)*

Chapter 57

Restoration

You can govern a nation with rules [a]

You can win a war with surprise tactics

But you can gain the entire world without interfering

How do I know this?

Because of this:

When there are many rules and restrictions [b]

More people become poor

When there are many sharp weapons [c]

More tragedy appears in the country

When there are many clever plans [d]

More cunning things occur

When there are many enforced laws [e]

More robbers and thieves appear

Therefore God says:

Be still [a]

And the people will transform themselves

Keep silent

And the people will rectify themselves

Do not interfere

And the people will enrich themselves

Surrender Earthly desires [f]

And the people will simplify themselves

[a] Psalm 37:6-10 *(He will make your vindication shine like the light, and the justice of your cause like the noonday. Be still before the Lord, and wait patiently for him; do not fret over those who prosper in their way, over those who carry out evil devices...)*

[b] Proverbs 28:2-3 *(When a land rebels it has many rulers; but with an intelligent ruler there is lasting order. A ruler who oppresses the poor is a beating rain that leaves no food.)*
Isaiah 10:1

[c] Psalm 37:14-15 *(The wicked draw the sword and bend their bows to bring down the poor and needy, to kill those who walk uprightly; their sword shall enter their own heart, and their bows shall be broken.)*

[d] Psalm 64:5-6 *(They hold fast to their evil purpose; they talk of laying snares secretly, thinking, "Who can see us? Who can search out our crimes? We have thought out a cunningly conceived plot." For the human heart and mind are deep.)*

[e] Psalm 50:16-20 *(But to the wicked God says: "What right have you to recite my statutes, or take my covenant on your lips? For you hate discipline, and you cast my words behind you. You make friends with a thief when you see one, and you keep company with adulterers...)*

[f] Colossians 3:5-11 *(Put to death, therefore, whatever in you is earthly: fornication, impurity, passion, evil desire, and greed [which is idolatry]. On account of these the wrath of God is coming on those who are disobedient. These are the ways you also once followed, when you were living that life. But now you must get rid of all such things - anger, wrath, malice, slander, and abusive language from your mouth. Do not lie to one another, seeing that you have stripped off the old self with its practices and have clothed yourselves with the new self, which is being renewed in knowledge according to the image of its creator...)*

Chapter 58
Paradox

When the country is ruled with a light hand [a]
The people lead simple and honest lives
When the country is ruled with an iron fist [b]
The people become shrewd and cunning

Misfortune is but the shadow of good fortune [c]
Good fortune is but the cloak of misfortune
Who knows when the last day will come? [d]

Is there any righteousness as it appears to be? [e]
What appears right develops into awkwardness
What appears good develops into evil
The people have long been confused by this

Thus, the wise are: [f]
Righteous without being condemning
Pointed without being piercing
Straightforward without being ruthless
Filled with light without being flashy

[a] John 13:12-17 *(After he had washed their feet, had put on his robe, and had returned to the table, he said to them, "Do you know what I have done to you? You call me Teacher and Lord - and you are right, for that is what I am. So if I, your Lord and Teacher, have washed your feet, you also out to wash one another's feet. For I have set you an example, that you also should do as I have done to you...)*

[b] Matthew 23:2-3 *("The scribes and Pharisees sit on Moses' seat; therefore do whatever they teach you and follow it; but do not do as they do, for they do not practice what they teach.)*
Matthew 23:15

[c] Matthew 19:30 *(But many who are first will be last, and the last will be first.)*
Job 8:7, Revelation 22:13

[d] Matthew 24:3-12 *(When he was sitting on the Mount of Olives, the disciples came to him privately, saying, "Tell us, when will this be, and what will be the sigh of your coming and of the end of the age?" Jesus answered them, "Beware that no one leads you astray. For many will come in my name, saying, 'I am the Messiah!' and they will lead many astray...)*
Matthew 24:36-37

[e] Isaiah 5:20 *(Ah, how you call evil good and good evil, who put darkness for light and light for darkness, who put bitter for sweet and sweet for bitter!)*
Romans 3:21-26, Matthew 24:24, Matthew 12:34

[f] 2 Corinthians 6:1-13 *(...We are treated as imposters, and yet are true; as unknown, and yet are well known; as dying, and see - we are alive; as punished, and yet not killed; as sorrowful, yet always rejoicing; as poor, yet making many rich; as having nothing, and yet possessing everything...)*

Chapter 59
Power of the Spirit

In governing men and serving Heaven [a]
There is nothing better than restraint
To manifest restraint is to surrender early from wasteful ideas

By surrendering early one accumulates the power of the Spirit [b]
The one who accumulates the power of the Spirit can overcome all things

If one can overcome all things [c]
Then anything is possible
If anything is possible
Then one can possess sovereignty

With the power of the Spirit [d]
One can endure for a long time
This is planting deep roots and building strong foundations
The Way of eternal life and lasting vision

[a] Psalm 37:7-13 *(…Refrain from anger, and forsake wrath. Do not fret - it only leads to evil. For the wicked shall be cut off, but those who wait for the Lord shall inherit the land…)*

[b] 2 Timothy 1:6-7 *(For this reason I remind you to rekindle the gift of God that is within you through the laying on of my hands; for God did not give us a spirit of cowardice, but rather a spirit of power and of love and self-discipline.)*
1 Corinthians 12:1-11

[c] Matthew 19:26 *(But Jesus looked at them and said, "For mortals it is impossible, but for God all things are possible.")*
Mark 9:23, John 14:11-14

[d] Galatians 6:8 *(If you sow to your own the flesh, you will reap corruption from the flesh; but if you sow to the Spirit, you will reap eternal life from the Spirit.)*
John 5:24, Luke 8:13-15

Chapter 60
Body of Light

Ruling a country is like cooking a small fish with care

When we rule according to the Word of God

Our inner darkness has no power to harm [a]

Not that inner darkness has no power [b]

But its power cannot harm a body filled with the light of God

Not only does it not harm [a]

The Master does not harm

Since neither is doing harm [c]

Oneness is restored for a common purpose

[a] John 8:12 *(Again Jesus spoke to them, saying, "I am the light of the world. Whoever follows me will never walk in darkness but will have the light of life.")*

[b] Luke 11:34-36 *(Your eye is the lamp of your body. If your eye is healthy, your whole body is full of light; but if it is not healthy, your body is full of darkness. Therefore consider whether the light in you is not darkness. If then your whole body is full of light, with no part of it in darkness, it will be as full of light as when a lamp gives you light with its rays.")*

[c] 1 Peter 5:6-11 *(Humble yourselves therefore under the mighty hand of God, so that he may exalt you in due time. Cast all your anxiety on him, because he cares for you. Discipline yourselves, keep alert. Like a roaring lion your adversary the devil prowls around, looking for someone to devour. Resist him, steadfast in your faith, for you know that your brothers and sisters in all the world are undergoing the same kinds of suffering. And after you have suffered for a little while, the God of all grace, who has called you to his eternal glory in Christ, will himself restore, support, strengthen, and establish you. To him be the power forever and ever. Amen.)*
Romans 12:14-21

Chapter 61
Honoring the Low

The great kingdom is like the low lands where rivers flow [a]
It is the central meeting-ground of the world
It is the female reservoir of the world

The masculine honors the feminine for her stillness [b]
She uses stillness to keep the lower position

Similarly, a great kingdom that takes the low place of a small
kingdom gains the honor of the smaller

Likewise, a small kingdom that remains in the low place gains the
honor of a great kingdom

One gains honor by taking the lowest place and the other gains
honor by remaining low

A great kingdom desires to grow the population it nourishes [c]
And a small kingdom desires to join by serving the greater

Both kingdoms achieve what they desire
Thus, whoever takes the lowest place will be honored by the other [b]

[a] Genesis 2:8-15 *(And the Lord God planted a garden in Eden, in the east; and there he put the man whom he had formed. Out of the ground the Lord God made to grow every tree that is pleasant to the sight and good for food, the tree of life also in the midst of the garden, and the tree of the knowledge of good and evil. A river flows out of Eden to water the garden, and from there it divides and becomes four branches. The name of the first is Pishon; it is the one that flows around the whole land of Havilah, where there is gold; and the gold of that land is good; bdellium and onyx stone are there. The name of the second river is Gihon; it is the one that flows around the whole land of Cush. The name of the third river is Tigris, which flows east of Assyria. And the fourth river is the Euphrates. The Lord God took the man and put him in the garden of Eden to till it and keep it.)*

[b] Luke 14:10-11 *(But when you are invited, go and sit down at the lowest place, so that when your host comes, he may say to you, 'Friend, move up higher'; then you will be honored in the presence of all who sit at the table with you. For all who exalt themselves will be humbled, and those who humble themselves will be exalted.")*

[c] Proverbs 14:28 *(The glory of a king is a multitude of people; without people a prince is ruined.)*

Chapter 62
Gift of Salvation

God is the author of all creation [a]
He is the treasure of the righteous [b]
And the refuge of the unrighteous

Good words can win people over [c]
Good deeds can bless people [d]

Even if we are faithless, He remains faithful [e]
For He cannot deny Himself

Hence, the Son of God is honored at the right hand of God [f]
And before the angels encircling the throne [g]

Though there is the offering of jade
Followed by stately horses
It does not compare to being seated in the kingdom of God

Why did our ancestors value God so highly?
They were told that those who seek will find [h]
And those who sin shall be set free [i]
Therefore, salvation is the greatest gift of God

[a] John 1:3-5 *(All things came into being through him, and without him not one thing came into being in him was life, and the life was the light of all people. The light shines in the darkness, and the darkness did not overcome it.)*

[b] Matthew 5:43-48 *(…But I say to you, love your enemies and pray for those who persecute you, so that you may be children of your Father in heaven; for he makes his sun rise on the evil and on the good, and sends rain on the righteous and on the unrighteous…)*
Colossians 1:13-14, Psalm 18:2, Psalm 18:30, Nahum 1:7

[c] Matthew 11:28-30 *("Come to me, all you that are weary and are carrying heavy burdens, and I will give you rest. Take my yoke upon you, and learn from me; for I am gentle and humble in heart, and you will find rest for your souls…)*
Hebrews 4:12

[d] Titus 2:7-9 *(Show yourself in all respects a model of good works, and in your teaching show integrity, gravity, and sound speech that cannot be censured; then any opponent will be put to shame, having nothing evil to say of us…)*
John 3:16-17

[e] 2 Timothy 2:11-13 *(The saying is sure: If we have died with him, we will also live with him; 12 if we endure, we will also reign with him; if we deny him, he will also deny us; 13 if we are faithless, he remains faithful— for he cannot deny himself.)*

[f] Matthew 26:64 *(Jesus said to him, "You have said so. But I tell you, from now on you will see the Son of Man seated at the right hand of Power and coming on the clouds of heaven.")*

[g] Revelation 7:11-12 *(And all the angels stood around the throne and around the elders and the four living creatures, and they fell on their faces before the throne and worshiped God,…)*

[h] Matthew 7:7-8 *("Ask, and it will be given you; search, and you will find; knock, and the door will be opened for you…)*

[i] Hebrews 9:27-28 *(And just as it is appointed for mortals to die once, and after that the judgment, so Christ, having been offered once to bear the sins of many, will appear a second time, not to deal with sin, but to save those who are eagerly awaiting him.)*
Romans 6:22

Chapter 63
Achieving Greatness

Act with stillness [a]
Work without effort [b]
Taste without engrossing [c]

Make great in what is small [d]
Make abundant in what is few [e]
Reward hatred with kindness [f]

See simplicity in difficult tasks [g]
Achieve greatness in small things

Difficult tasks of the world are handled through the simple tasks
Large tasks of the world are handled through the small tasks
Therefore, the wise do not need to handle large tasks
Any yet they still achieve greatness

People who make promises lightly are not trustworthy [h]
People who take everything too lightly encounter more difficulties

Therefore, the wise identify the task as difficult
So they do not encounter difficulties

[a] Psalm 46:10 *("Be still, and know that I am God! I am exalted among the nations, I am exalted in the earth.")*
Psalm 37:5-7

[b] John 14:10 *(Do you not believe that I am in the Father and the Father is in me? The words that I say to you I do not speak on my own; but the Father who dwells in me does his works.)*

[c] Luke 18:22 *(When Jesus heard this, he said to him, "There is still one thing lacking. Sell all that you own and distribute the money to the poor, and you will have treasure in heaven; then come, follow me.")*
1 Corinthians 7:29-31

[d] Genesis 12:1-2 *(Now the Lord said to Abram, "Go from your country and your kindred and your father's house to the land that I will show you. I will make of you a great nation, and I will bless you, and make your name great, so that you will be a blessing.)*

[e] James 2:5 *(Listen, my beloved brothers and sisters. Has not God chosen the poor in the world to be rich in faith and to be heirs of the kingdom that he has promised to those who love him?)*

[f] Matthew 5:43-48 *("You have heard that it was said, 'You shall love your neighbor and hate your enemy.' But I say to you, love your enemies and pray for those who persecute you,…)*

[g] Matthew 17:20 *(He said to them, "Because of your little faith. For truly I tell you, if you have faith the size of a mustard seed, you will say to this mountain, "Move from here to there,' and it will move; and nothing will be impossible for you.")*
James 3:3-10

[h] Proverbs 20:25 *(It is a snare for one to say rashly, "It is holy," and begin to reflect only after making a vow.)*
Psalm 146:1-5, Psalm 119:67, Jeremiah 9:4-9

Chapter 64

Journey of Faith

When things are still and quiet, situations are easy to control [a]
When there are yet no problems, it is easy to plan [b]
When things are fragile, they can easily break
When matters are small, they can easily scatter

Prepare before problems begin [b]
Get things in order before they get out of hand

A tree trunk as wide as a man's arm span grows from a seedling [c]
A tower nine stories high begins with a mound of earth
A journey of a thousand miles begins with a footprint
    beneath the feet

Those who interfere will fail [a]
Those who find their life according to this world will lose it [d]

Thus, the wise do not interfere [a]
And yet they never fail
They do not find life according to this world [d]
And yet never lose it

In handling affairs, people often fail at the point of success [d]
Keep the faith to the end no less than at the beginning [e]
And the journey will have no failure

The wise do not desire what men desire [d]
They do not store up treasures of this world
They learn to be rid of worldly knowledge [f]
They redeem us from what was lost [d]
They restore the nature of all things [e]
They can do this without interfering

[a] Psalm 23:1-3 *(The Lord is my shepherd, I shall not want. He makes me lie down in green pastures; he leads me beside still waters; he restores my soul. He leads me in right paths for his name's sake.)*
Psalm 37:5-7, Psalm 55:22, Psalm 62:5

[b] Proverbs 4:10-15 *(Hear, my child, and accept my words, that the years of your life may be many. I have taught you the way of wisdom; I have led you in the paths of uprightness. When you walk, your step will not be hampered; and if you run, you will not stumble...)*
Proverbs 3:5-6

[c] Habakkuk 2:3 *(For there is still a vision for the appointed time; it speaks of the end, and does not lie. If it seems to tarry, wait for it; it will surely come, it will not delay.)*
Genesis 12:1-2

[d] Matthew 10:38-39 *(...and whoever does not take up the cross and follow me is not worthy of me. Those who find their life will lose it, and those who lose their life for my sake will find it.)*
Proverbs 28:20, Matthew 4:8-11, 1 Timothy 6:10, Luke 12:13-21, Romans 8:5

[e] Titus 2:11-15 *(For the grace of God has appeared, bringing salvation to all, training us to renounce impiety and worldly passions, and in the present age to live lives that are self-controlled, upright, and godly, while we wait for the blessed hope and the manifestation of the glory of our great God and Savior, Jesus Christ...)*
Matthew 17:20, John 16:33, Matthew 11:29

[f] 1 Corinthians 2:6-7 *(Yet among the mature we do speak wisdom, though it is not a wisdom of this age or of the rulers of this age, who are doomed to perish. But we speak God's wisdom, secret and hidden, which God decreed before the ages for our glory.)*
Colossians 1:9, James 1:5

Chapter 65
Excessive Cleverness

In ancient times, devout messengers of God used their wisdom not
to enlighten people
But rather to be the way and the truth and the life [a]

People become difficult to govern [b]
Due to their excessive cleverness

Therefore, governing people with cleverness
Brings thieves among the people

Governing people without cleverness
Brings blessings upon the people

Know these two basic principles [a]
Forever knowing these principles
Is profound understanding of the Mystic Spirit

The Mystic Spirit runs deep-penetrating and far-reaching [c]
It returns all things to their natural state of perfect harmony [d]

[a] 1 Corinthians 1:20-25 *(Where is the one who is wise? Where is the scribe? Where is the debater of this age? Has not God made foolish the wisdom of the world? For since, in the wisdom of God, the world did not know God through wisdom, God decided, through the foolishness of our proclamation, to save those who believe. For Jews demand signs and Greeks desire wisdom, but we proclaim Christ crucified, a stumbling block to Jews and foolishness to Gentiles, but to those who are the called, both Jews and Greeks, Christ the power of God and the wisdom of God. For God's foolishness is wiser than human wisdom, and God's weakness is stronger than human strength.)*
1 Corinthians 2:6-16, 1 Corinthians 3:19, John 14:6

[b] Matthew 23:1-7 *(Then Jesus said to the crowds and to his disciples, "The scribes and the Pharisees sit on Moses' seat; therefore, do whatever they teach you and follow it; but do not do as they do, for they do not practice what they teach. They tie up heavy burdens, hard to bear, and lay them on the shoulders of others; but they themselves are unwilling to lift a finger to move them...)*

[c] 1 Corinthians 2:9-11 *(But, as it is written, "What no eye has seen nor ear heard, nor the human heart conceived, what God has prepared for those who love him" - these things God has revealed to us through the Spirit; for the Spirit searches everything, even the depths of God. For what human being knows what is truly human except the human spirit that is within? So also no one comprehends what is truly God's except the Spirit of God.)*

[d] Hebrews 12:22-24 *(But you have come to Mount Zion and to the city of the living God, the heavenly Jerusalem, and to innumerable angels in festal gathering, and to the assembly of the firstborn who are enrolled in heaven, and to God the judge of all, and to the spirits of the righteous made perfect, and to Jesus, the mediator of a new covenant, and to the sprinkled blood that speaks a better word than the blood of Abel.)*
John 16:13

Chapter 66
Leading From Behind

Rivers and oceans are like kings of a hundred valleys [a]
Because they are good at taking the lowest place
Thus they are like kings of a hundred valleys

If you want to be the Master [b]
You must become the Servant

If you want to be first [c]
You must place yourself last

Thus when the Son was deemed Master [d]
The people did not feel burdened

And when the Son was positioned first
The people did not feel harmed

Therefore, the people joyfully glorified Him without getting
tired of Him

Do not compete [e]
And competition will not meet you

[a] Luke 14:10-11 *(But when you are invited, go and sit down at the lowest place, so that when your host comes, he may say to you, 'Friend, move up higher'; then you will be honored in the presence of all who sit at the table with you. For all who exalt themselves will be humbled, and those who humble themselves will be exalted.")*

[b] John 13:12-17 *(After he had washed their feet, had put on his robe, and had returned to the table, he said to them, "Do you know what I have done to you? You call me Teacher and Lord - and you are right, for that is what I am. So if I, your Lord and Teacher, have washed your feet, you also ought to wash one another's feet. For I have set you an example, that you also should do as I have done to you. Very truly, I tell you, servants are not greater than their master, nor are messengers greater than the one who sent them. If you know these things, you are blessed if you do them.)*

[c] Mark 9:35 *(He sat down, called the twelve, and said to them, "Whoever wants to be first must be last of all and servant of all.")*

[d] 1 Thessalonians 1:2-7 *(...For we know, brothers and sisters beloved by God, that he has chosen you, because our message of the gospel came to you not in word only, but also in power and in the Holy Spirit and with full conviction ...And you became imitators of us and of the Lord, for in spite of persecution you received the word with joy in inspired by the Holy Spirit, so that you became an example to all the believers in Macedonia and in Achaia.)*
Acts 20:24

[e] Philippians 2:3-4 *(Do nothing from selfish ambition or conceit, but in humility regard others as better than yourselves. Let each of you look not to your own interests, but to the interest of others.)*
Galatians 6:4

Chapter 67
Power of Love

The whole world says God is Great [a]
As if He is beyond compare
Because of God's Greatness
He seems beyond compare
If God can be compared
He would have been forgotten long ago

I have three treasures I hold and protect [b]

The first is love
The second is moderation
And the third is humility

Knowing love one becomes fearless [c]
Knowing moderation one becomes generous [d]
Knowing humility one gets ahead [e]

If one is fearless but abandons love [f]
Generous but abandons moderation
And gets ahead but abandons humility
This will surely lead to death

Use love when engaging in battle and all will be conquered [g]
And our defense will be secured
Love is the means by which the Heavens protect and save

[a] Job 36:22-33 *(…Surely God is great, and we do not know him; the number of his years is unsearchable. For he draws up the drops of water; he distills his mist in rain which the skies pour down and drop upon mortals abundantly…)*
Psalm 113:1-2

[b] 1 Corinthians 13:4-13 *(Love is patient; love is kind; love is not envious or boastful or arrogant or rude…And now faith, hope, and love abide, these three; and the greatest of these is love.)*
Colossians 3:12, Galatians 5:22-23

[c] 1 John 4:18 *(There is no fear in love, but perfect love casts our fear; for fear has to do with punishment, and whoever fears has not reached perfection in love.)*

[d] Luke 12:32-34 *("Do not be afraid, little flock, for it is your Father's good pleasure to give you the kingdom. Sell your possessions, and give alms. Make purses for yourselves that do not wear out, an unfailing treasure in heaven, where no thief comes near and no moth destroys. For where your treasure is, there your heart is also.)*

[e] Luke 14:10-11 *(But when you are invited, go and sit down at the lowest place, so that when your host comes, he may say to you, 'Friend, move up higher'; then you will be honored in the presence of all who sit at the table with you. For all who exalt themselves will be humbled, and those who humble themselves will be exalted.")*

[f] Proverbs 14:12 *(There is a way that seems right to a person, but its end is the way to death.)*

[g] Romans 8:28-38 *(We know that all things work together for good for those who love God, who are called according to his purpose. For those whom he foreknew he also predestined to be conformed to the image of his Son, on order that he might be the first born within a large family…)*

Chapter 68
Spiritual Unity

Good generals are not warlike [a]
Good warriors do not get angry
Those who are good defeat their opponent without engaging them
Those who are good humble themselves before the people

It is called the virtue of not contending [b]
It is called the power to use the strength of others
It is called being One with the Heavenly Spirit
The great principle of old

[a] Psalm 37:1-9 *(Do not fret because of the wicked; do not be envious of wrongdoers, for they will soon fade like the grass, and wither like the green herb. Trust in the Lord, and do good; so you will live in the land, and enjoy security. Take delight in the Lord, and he will give you the desires of your heart. Commit your way to the Lord; trust in him, and he will act. He will make your vindication shine like the light, and the justice of your cause like the noonday. Be still before the Lord, and wait patiently for him; do not fret over those who prosper in their way, over those who carry out evil devices. Refrain from anger, and forsake wrath. Do not fret - it leads only to evil. For the wicked shall be cut off, but those who wait for the Lord shall inherit the land.)*
Matthew 26:50-56

[b] Ephesians 3:16-21 *(I pray that, according to the riches of his glory, he may grant that you may be strengthened in your inner being with power through his Spirit, and that Christ may dwell in your hearts through faith, as you are being rooted and grounded in love. I pray that you may have the power to comprehend, with all the saints, what is the breadth and length and height and depth, and to know the love of Christ that surpasses knowledge, so that you may be filled with all the fullness of God. Now to him who by the power at work within us is able to accomplish abundantly far more than all we can ask or imagine, to him be glory in the church and in Christ Jesus to all generations, forever and ever. Amen.)*
Romans 8:9-11, Colossians 1:11-12

Chapter 69

Compassion

There is a military saying: [a]
I prefer not to attack but rather to be still
I prefer not to advance an inch but rather to retreat a foot

This is advancing without moving forward [a]
Rolling up one's sleeves without baring one's arms
Engaging the enemy without confrontation
Fully armed without any weapons

There is no greater disaster than to underestimate the
    power of an enemy [b]
Underestimating the power of my enemy nearly made me
    lose my treasures

Therefore, when evenly opposing forces meet [a]
The victory will go to the compassionate side that yields [c]

[a] Exodus 14:13-18 *(But Moses said to the people, "Do not be afraid, stand firm, and see the deliverance that the Lord will accomplish for you today; for the Egyptians whom you see today you shall never see again. The Lord will fight for you, and you have only to keep still." Then the Lord said to Moses, "Why do you cry out to me? Tell the Israelites to go forward. But you lift up your staff, and stretch out your hand over the sea and divide it, that the Israelites may go into the sea on dry ground. Then I will harden the hearts of the Egyptians so that they will go in after them, and so I will gain glory for myself over Pharoah and all his army, his chariots, and his chariot drivers. And the Egyptians shall know that I am the Lord, when I have gained glory for myself over Pharoah, his chariots and his chariot drivers.")*
Psalm 37:7, Proverbs 14:16-17, Psalm 46:9-11, Matthew 5:43-48

[b] 1 Peter 5:8-9 *(Discipline yourselves, keep alert. Like a roaring lion your adversary the devil prowls around, looking for someone to devour. Resist him, steadfast in your faith, for you know that your brothers and sisters in all the world are undergoing the same kinds of suffering.)*
Ephesians 6:12, 2 Corinthians 11:3

[c] Isaiah 63:8-9 *(For he said, "Surely they are my people, children who will not deal falsely"; and he became their savior in all their distress. It was no messenger or angel but his presence that saved them; in his love and in his pity he redeemed them; he lifted them up and carried them all the days of old.)*
Hebrews 2:17

Chapter 70
Understanding God

My words are easy to understand and easy to follow [a]
Yet, the world does not understand and does not follow

My words are from the beginning of time [b]
My actions come from the One who sent me [c]
If people do not know this, they do not know me [d]

Those who understand me are few [a]
But it does not lessen my worth

Though the Son of God wears the rough clothes of a servant [e]
He carries a priceless treasure in His heart

[a] Matthew 13:10-17 *(Then the disciples came and asked him, "Why do you speak to them in parables?" He answered, "To you it has been given to know the secrets of the kingdom of heaven, but to them it has not been given. For to those who have, more will be given, and they will have an abundance; but from those who have nothing, even what they have will be taken away. The reason I speak to them in parables is that 'seeing they do not perceive, and hearing they do not listen, nor do they understand. With them indeed is fulfilled the prophecy of Isaiah that says: 'You will indeed listen, but never understand, and you will indeed look, but never perceive. For this people's heart has grown dull, and their ears are hard of hearing, and they have shut their eyes; so that they might not look with their eyes, and listen with their ears, and understand with their heart, and turn - and I would heal them.'...)*

[b] John 1:1-2 *(In the beginning was the Word, and the Word was with God, and the Word was God. He was in the beginning with God.)*

[c] John 14:10 *(Do you not believe that I am in the Father and the Father is in me? The words that I say to you I do not speak on my own; but the Father who dwells in me does his works.)*
John 5:30

[d] John 5:45-47 *(Do not think that I will accuse you before the Father; your accuser is Moses, on whom you have set your hope. If you believed Moses, you would believe me, for he wrote about me. But if you do not believe what he wrote, how will you believe what I say?")*
John 8:39-40

[e] Matthew 6:19-21 *("Do not store up for yourselves treasures on earth, where moth and rust consume and where thieves break in and steal; but store up for yourselves treasures in heaven, where neither moth nor rust consumes and where thieves do not break in and steal. For where your treasure is, there your heart will be also.)*

Chapter 71
Knowing Sin

To know that you do not know is wisdom [a]
To not know but proclaim that you know is sin

When one recognizes sin as a sin [b]
One can be free from sin

The Son of God is without sin [c]
Because He recognizes sin as sin [d]
That is why He is free from sin

[a] Matthew 23:1-4 *(Then Jesus said to the crowds and to his disciples, "The scribes and Pharisees sit on Moses' seat; therefore, do whatever they teach you and follow it; but do not do as they do, for they do not practice what they teach. They tie up heavy burdens, hard to bear, and lay them on the shoulders of others; but they themselves are unwilling to lift a finger to move them)*
1 John 1:8, John 9:41, Job 36:26

[b] Romans 6:15-18 *(What then? Should we sin because we are not under law but under grace? By no means! Do you not know that if you present yourselves to anyone as obedient slaves, you are slaves of the one whom you obey, either of sin, which leads to death, or of obedience, which leads to righteousness? But thanks be to God that you, having once been slaves of sin, have become obedient from the heart to the form of teaching to which you were entrusted, and that you, having been set free from sin, have become slaves of righteousness.)*

[c] 1 Peter 2:22-24 *("He committed no sin, and no deceit was found in his mouth." When he was abused, he did not return abuse; when he suffered, he did not threaten; but he entrusted himself to the one who judges justly. He himself bore our sins in his body on the cross, so that, free from sins, we might live for righteousness; by his wounds you have been healed.)*
1 John 3:4-6, 2 Corinthians 5:21

[d] Romans 8:1-8 *(There is therefore now no condemnation for those who are in Christ Jesus. For the law of the Spirit of life in Christ Jesus has set you free from the law of sin and of death. For God has done what the law, weakened by the flesh, could not do: by sending his own Son in the likeness of sinful flesh, and to deal with sin, he condemned sin in the flesh, so that the just requirement of the law might be fulfilled in us, who walk not according to the flesh but according to the Spirit...)*

Chapter 72
Freedom

When people have nothing to fear [a]
A greater force will rise

Do not confine people within narrow walls [b]
Do not burden their livelihood

If you do not despise them [c]
Then they will not despise you

Therefore the wise:
Know themselves but do not glorify [d]
Value themselves but do not boast [e]
Thus, they disregard one and choose the other

[a] Exodus 7:1-16 *(The Lord said to Moses, "See, I have made you like God to Pharoah, and your brother Aaron shall be your prophet. You shall speak all that I command you, and your brother Aaron shall tell Pharoah to let the Israelites go out of this land. But I will harden Pharoah's heart, and I will multiply my signs and wonders in the land of Egypt. When Pharoah does not listen to you, I will lay my hand upon Egypt and bring my people the Israelites, company by company, out of the land of Egypt by great acts of judgment. The Egyptians shall know that I am the Lord, when I stretch out my hand against Egypt and bring the Israelites out from among them."...)*

[b] Exodus 1:1-22 *(...But the more they were oppressed, the more they multiplied and spread, so that the Egyptians came to dread the Israelites. The Egyptians became ruthless in imposing tasks on the Israelites, and made their lives bitter with hard service in mortar and brick and in every kind of field labor. They were ruthless in all the tasks that they imposed on them...)*

[c] Luke 6:31 *(Do to others as you would have them do to you.)*

[d] John 8:54-56 *(Jesus answered, "If I glorify myself, my glory is nothing. It is my Father who glorifies me, he of whom you say, 'He is our God,' though you do not know him. But I do know him; if I would say that I do not know him, I would be a liar like you. But I do know him and I keep his word. Your ancestor Abraham rejoiced that he would see my day; he saw it and was glad.")*

[e] Luke 14:11 *(For all who exalt themselves will be humbled, and those who humble themselves will be exalted.")*

Chapter 73
Judgment of God

The bold who are brave will die by the sword [a]
The bold who are careful will live
Of these two, one gains and the other loses [b]

One is not favored by Heaven [b]
Who knows the reason?
Even the wise find this difficult [c]

The God of Heaven:
Conquers without contending [d]
Responds without speaking [e]
Cannot be summoned and yet is present [f]
Does not rush things and yet fulfills [g]

The Heavenly net is wide and vast [h]
And yet nobody can slip through it [i]

[a] Matthew 26:51-54 *(Suddenly, one of those with Jesus put his hand on his sword, drew it, and struck the slave of the high priest, cutting off his ear. Then Jesus said to him, "Put your sword back into its place; for all who take the sword will perish by the sword…)*

[b] Luke 9:23-25 *(Then he said to them all, "If any want to become my followers, let them deny themselves and take up their cross daily and follow me. For those who want to save their life will lose it, and those who lose their life for my sake will save it…)*

[c] Matthew 5:43-48 *("You have heard that it was said, 'You shall love your neighbor and hate your enemy.' But I say to you, Love your enemies and pray for those who persecute you,…)*

[d] Psalm 46:10-11 *("Be still, and know that I am God! I am exalted among the nations, I am exalted in the earth"…)*
Hebrews 11:30, Exodus 14:14

[e] 1 Kings 19:11-12 *(He said, "Go out and stand on the mountain before the Lord, for the Lord is about to pass by…and after the fire a sound of sheer silence.)*

[f] 1 Corinthians 5:3-4 *(For though absent in body, I am present in spirit; and as if present I have already pronounced judgment in the name of the Lord Jesus on the man who has done such a thing. When you are assembled, and my spirit is present with the power of our Lord Jesus,…)*
John 3:8

[g] Psalm 27:14 *(Wait for the Lord; be strong, and let your heart take courage; wait for the Lord!)*
Psalm 33:20, 2 Peter 3:9

[h] Isaiah 42:5 *(Thus says God, the Lord, who created the heavens and stretched them out, who spread out the earth and what comes from it, who gives breath to the people upon it:…)*
Deuteronomy 10:14

[i] Romans 14:10-12 *(…For it is written, "As I live, says the Lord, every knee shall bow to me, and every tongue shall give praise to God." So then, each of us will be accountable to God.)*
Revelation 20:11-15, Nahum 1:3

Chapter 74

The Sovereign Judge

If people do not fear death [a]

Why should you threaten them with death?

If people live in constant fear of death

And you can kill the evildoers

Who would dare to do it?

Let the sovereign God be the judge according to our sins [b]

To take the place of God

Is like trying to cut for the master carpenter

If you try to cut for the master carpenter

You will end up cutting off your hand

[a] 2 Timothy 4:6-8 *(As for me, I am already being poured out as a libation, and the time of my departure has come. I have fought the good fight, I have finished the race, I have kept the faith. From now on there is reserved for me the crown of righteousness, which the Lord, the righteous judge, will give me on that day, and not only to me but also to all who have longed for his appearing.)*

[b] 1 Corinthians 4:5 *(Therefore do not pronounce judgment before the time, before the Lord comes, who will bring to light the things now hidden in darkness and will disclose the purposes of the heart. Then each one will receive commendation from God.)*
Psalm 96:13, Romans 14:1-12, Matthew 7:1-5

Chapter 75
Materialism

People suffer from famine [a]
Because their rulers enforce heavy taxation
That is why they starve

People are difficult to govern [b]
Because their rulers interfere too much
That is why they are difficult to govern

People think little of death [c]
Because their rulers demand too much of life
That is why they think little of death

The treasures of life are gained by those who let go [d]
And missed by those who hold on

[a] Luke 6:24-25 *("But woe to you who are rich, for you have received your consolation. Woe to you who are full now, for you will be hungry. Woe to you who are laughing now, for you will mourn and weep.)*
Psalm 49:12

[b] Exodus 5:1-9 *(Afterward Moses and Aaron went to Pharoah and said, "Thus says the Lord, the God of Israel, 'Let my people go, so that they may celebrate a festival to me in the wilderness.'" But Pharoah said, "Who is the Lord, that I should heed him and let Israel go? I do not know the Lord, and I will not let Israel go."...)*

[c] Philippians 1:20-21 *(It is my eager expectation and hope that I will not be put to shame in any way, but that by my speaking with all boldness, Christ will be exalted now as always in my body, whether by life or by death. For to me, living is Christ and dying is gain.)*
Galatians 2:19-21, Romans 8:13, Romans 14:7-9, 1 John 2:15-17

[d] Matthew 6:19-21 *("Do not store up for yourselves treasures on earth, where moth and rust consume and where thieves break in and steal; but store up for yourselves treasures in heaven, where neither moth nor rust consumes and where thieves do not break in and steal. For where your treasure is, there you heart will be also.)*
Matthew 6:24, Matthew 16:25-26

Chapter 76
Soft and Hard

People begin life soft and tender [a]
At death they end up hard and rigid

Trees and grass begin life soft and supple
At death they end up hard and brittle

Hence the hard and inflexible are followers of the dead
And the soft and yielding are followers of the living

Thus, the inflexible and unyielding army will fall [b]
    by their own weight
Just as hard wood will be cut down

The hard and inflexible will occupy the Earth below
While the soft and yielding will inherit the Earth above

[a] 1 Peter 2:1-3 *(Rid yourselves, therefore, of all malice, and all guile, insincerity, envy, and all slander. Like newborn infants, long for the pure, spiritual milk, so that by it you may grow into salvation - if indeed you have tasted that the Lord is good.)*
Proverbs 11:19

[b] Psalm 37:8-13 *(Refrain from anger, and forsake wrath. Do not fret - it leads only to evil. For the wicked shall be cut off, but those who wait for the Lord shall inherit the land. Yet a little while, and the wicked will be no more; though you look diligently for their place, they will not be there. But the meek shall inherit the land, and delight themselves in abundant prosperity. The wicked plot against the righteous, and gnash their teeth against them; but the Lord laughs at the wicked, for he sees that their day is coming.)*
Proverbs 11:5, Proverbs 28:10

Chapter 77
Equality

The God of Heaven is like drawing a bow [a]
The top end bends down to a lower position
The bottom end bends up to a higher position
Reduce the draw if it is too much [b]
Add to the draw if it is too little

The Heavenly Way of God [b]
Reduces from what is too much
In order to add to what is too little

The way of people is different [c]
They reduce from what is too little
In order to add to what is too much

Who can offer their excess to serve the world? [d]
Only those who have the Spirit of God

Therefore, they fulfill their purpose without recognition [e]
Achieve without taking credit
And do not wish to glorify their good works

[a] Luke 14:8-11 *(...But when you are invited, go and sit down at the lowest place, so that when your host comes, he may say to you, 'Friend, move up higher'; then you will be honored in the presence of all who sit at the table with you. For all who exalt themselves will be humbled, and those who humble themselves will be exalted.")*

[b] 1 Samuel 2:7-8 *(The Lord makes poor and makes rich; he brings low, he also exalts. He raises up the poor from the dust; he lifts the needy from the ash heap, to make them sit with princes and inherit a seat of honor. For the pillars of the earth are the Lord's, and on them he has set the world.)* Proverbs 13:7, 2 Corinthians 8:9

[c] James 2:1-5 *(My brothers and sisters, do you with your acts of favoritism really believe in our glorious Lord Jesus Christ? For if a person with gold rings and in fine clothes comes into your assembly, and if a poor person in dirty clothes also comes in, and if you take notice of the one wearing the fine clothes and say, "Have a seat here, please," while to the one who is poor you say, "Stand there," or, "Sit at my feet," have you not made distinctions among yourselves, and become judges with evil thoughts? ...)* Proverbs 22:16, Proverbs 28:27

[d] John 14:10-12 *(Do you not believe that I am in the Father and the Father is in me? The words that I say to you I do not speak on my own; but the Father who dwells in me does his works. Believe me that I am in the Father and the Father is in me; but if you do not, then believe me because of the works themselves...)*

[e] John 8:54-55 *(Jesus answered, "If I glorify myself, my glory is nothing. It is my Father who glorifies me, he of whom you say, 'He is our God,' though you do not know him. But I know him; if I would say that I do not know him I would be a liar like you. But I do know him and I keep his word.)*

Chapter 78
Strength in Weakness

Nothing in the world is weaker and softer than water [a]
Yet, nothing is more powerful at breaking up the strong and hard
There is no substitute

The weak overcomes the strong [a]
The soft overcomes the hard
Everyone knows this but they have no desire to practice it

Therefore, the wise man says:
The Son became sin for us [b]
Thus, He is fit to be Master
The Son bore the woes of the world [c]
Thus, He is fit to be King of the World

The truth often sounds paradoxical [d]

[a] 2 Corinthians 12:8-10 *(Three times I appealed to the Lord about this, that it would leave me, but he said to me, "My grace is sufficient for you, for power is made perfect in weakness." So, I will boast all the more gladly of my weaknesses, so that the power of Christ may dwell in me. Therefore, I am content with weaknesses, insults, hardships, persecutions, and calamities for the sake of Christ; for whenever I am weak, then I am strong.)*
1 Corinthians 1:27

[b] 2 Corinthians 5:21 *(For our sake he made him to be sin who knew no sin, so that in him we might become the righteousness of God.)*
1 John 2:2

[c] Revelation 5:11-14 *(…singing with full voice, "Worthy is the Lamb that was slaughtered to receive power and wealth and wisdom and might and honor and glory and blessings!" Then I heard every creature in heaven and on earth and under the earth and in the sea, and all that is in them, singing, "To the one seated on the throne and to the Lamb be blessing and honor and glory and might forever and ever!" And the four living creatures said, "Amen!" And the elders fell down and worshiped.)*

[d] Mark 8:35 *(For those who want to save their life will lose it, and those who lose their life for my sake, and for the sake of the gospel, will save it.)*

Chapter 79
Forgiving Debt

After settling a bitter dispute [a]
Some resentment remains
How can this be good?

The righteous man upholds his half of the bargain [a]
But does not demand anything from the other

The righteous fulfill their obligations [a]
But the unrighteous demand compensation

Though our Heavenly God is impartial, [b]
He gives to those who serve others [c]

[a] Luke 6:27-36 *("But I say to you that listen, Love your enemies, do good to those who hate you, bless those who curse you, pray for those who abuse you. If anyone strikes you on the cheek, offer the other also; and from anyone who takes away your coat do not withhold even your shirt. Give to everyone who begs from you; and if anyone takes away your goods, do not ask for them again. Do to others as you would have them do to you. If you love those who love you, what credit is that to you? For even sinners love those who love them. If you do good to those who do good to you, what credit is that to you? For even sinners do the same. If you lend to those from whom you hope to receive, what credit is that to you? Even sinners lend to sinners to receive as much again. But love your enemies, do good and lend, expecting nothing in return. Your reward will be great, and you will be children of the Most High; for he is kind to the ungrateful and the wicked. Be merciful just as your Father is merciful.")*

[b] 1 Peter 1:17 *(If you invoke as Father the one who judges all people impartially according to their deeds, live in reverent fear during the time of your exile.)*
Romans 2:11

[c] Proverbs 12:2 *(The good obtain favor from the Lord, but those who devise evil he condemns.)*
Proverbs 22:1

Chapter 80
Simple Life

Imagine a small country with a few people

They have labor-saving machines [a]
But do not use them

They take death seriously
So they do not risk life by traveling far

They have boats and carriages
But do not ride away in them

They have armor and weapons
But have no need for them

They return to their simple ways tying knots

They find their plain food pleasant
And their simple clothes fine

They are content in their homes
And enjoy their traditions

Even though their neighboring countries are close
And the roosters and dogs can be heard across the way

The people leave each other in peace to grow old and die [b]
Without ever visiting trouble between them

[a] Matthew 6:25-34 *("Therefore I tell you, do not worry about your life, what you will eat or what you will drink, or about your body, what you will wear. Is not life more than food, and the body more than clothing? Look at the birds of the air; the neither sow nor reap not gather into barns, and yet your heavenly Father feeds them. Are you not of more value than they? And can any of you by worrying add a single hour to your span of life? And why do you worry about clothing? Consider the lilies of the field, how they grow; they neither toil not spin, yet I tell you, even Solomon in all his glory was not clothed like one of these. But if God so clothes the grass of the fields, which is alive today and tomorrow is thrown into the oven, will he not much more clothe you - you of little faith? Therefore, do not worry, saying, 'What will we eat?' or 'What will we drink?' or 'What will we wear?' For it is the Gentles who strive for all these things; and indeed your heavenly Father knows that you need all these things. But strive first for the kingdom of God, and his righteousness, and all these things will be given to you as well. "So do not worry about tomorrow, for tomorrow will bring worries of its own. Today's trouble is enough for today.)*

[b] 1 Kings 5:4 *(But now the Lord my God has given me rest on every side; there is neither adversary nor misfortune.)*

Chapter 81
True Servants of God

Truthful words may not be beautiful [a]
Beautiful words may not be truthful
The righteous do not have the need to argue [b]
Those who have the need to argue are the unrighteous

Those who think they know much are not wise [c]
Those who think they are wise do not know much

The wise Master does not store up treasures on earth [d]
The more he serves, the more blessings he receives
The more he gives, the more abundant he becomes

The Way of Heaven benefits all and does not harm [e]
The way of the wise is to fulfill their duty without contending

[a] Galatians 4:16-17 *(Have I now become your enemy by telling you the truth? They make much of you, but for no good purpose; they want to exclude you, so that you may make much of them.)*

[b] Matthew 27:11-14 *(Now Jesus stood before the governor; and the governor asked him, "Are you the King of the Jews?" Jesus said, "You say so." But when he was accused by the chief priests and elders, he did not answer. Then Pilate said to him, "Do you not hear how many accusations they make against you?" But he gave him no answer, not even to a single charge, so that the governor was greatly amazed.)*
Luke 12:11-12

[c] 1 Corinthians 3:18-23 *(Do not deceive yourselves. If you think that you are wise in this age, you should become fools so that you may become wise. For the wisdom of this world is foolishness with God. For it is written, "He catches the wise in their craftiness," and again, "The Lord knows the thoughts of the wise, that they are futile." So let no one boast about human leaders. For all things are yours,…)*

[d] Luke 12:29-33 *(And do not keep striving for what you are to eat and what you are to drink, and do not keep worrying. For it is the nations of the world that strive after all these things, and your Father knows that you need them. Instead, strive for his kingdom, and these things will be given to you as well. Do not be afraid, little flock, for it is your Father's good pleasure to give you the kingdom...)*
Matthew 6:19-21, Proverbs 15:6

[e] Matthew 11:28-30 *("Come to me, all you that are weary and are carrying heavy burdens, and I will give you rest. Take up my yoke upon you, and learn from me; for I am gentle and humble in heart, and you will find rest for your souls. For my yoke is easy, and my burden is light.")*
Romans 8:28-31

BUILT FOR GREATNESS

We would love to hear about your 81-day journey.

Please email us at info@builtforgreatness.com

Visit www.builtforgreatness.com

Acknowledgments

I would like to give my deepest gratitude to the people who blessed me in countless ways and helped make my journey easier as I completed this book. As the process unfolded, I made friendships that taught me the meaning of love. I am indebted to all of you for giving me your time and support.

To God: I am deeply grateful and humbled knowing that You allowed me to write this book. I have failed You countless times and put other things before You, but You never once turned away. Now I hope to bring honor to You and to share Your Word to the world.

To the Virgin Mary: Thank you for interceding in my life on the night I met Richard at St. Vincent de Paul Church in Los Angeles. Your presence in my heart at the church garden was so powerful; it gave me a new outlook on life. Thank you for your love and continued prayers.

I am truly grateful to be married to Tracy Hoang, who has loved and supported me for over three decades now. She has continually put up with my outrageous business adventures and far-reaching dreams—including this project, which has consumed my life for the past ten years. Her love, patience, and care for me and for our five children can only be felt in my heart, not expressed in words. Tracy is the pillar and force behind all the dreams I have ever hoped for in life.

I would like to give special thanks to my parents, who have always loved me unconditionally. Their loving support is a great example of what I hope to provide for my children, and it has given me confidence to believe that anything is possible. Mom and Dad, I love you!

Acknowledgments

A very special thanks goes to my grandmother Nhu Pham, who helped raise me to become a faithful servant of God. Even though I didn't understand the Bible stories she shared with me when I was young, she planted the seed of the Gospel early in my life. I wish that I had finished this book before God welcomed her into heaven, but I know she is smiling down on me. Grandmother, don't forget the silver key you gave me years ago to open the gates of heaven. I still keep it close to me and will use it when I take my last breath. Grandmother, I love you!

Meeting Archbishop Sylvain Lavoie was miraculous and one of my greatest blessings. His energy and amazing spirit reminds me that anything is possible with God. It is truly a blessing we are working together to build the Kingdom of God. Hallelujah!

I am grateful to have the support of Archbishop José H. Gómez and Fr. Brian Nunes from the Archdiocese of Los Angeles who gave me their blessings and prayers to build the Kingdom of God. Thank you for the guidance, countless meetings, and infinite love. Amen!

I also thank Father John Tran from St. Lawrence Martyr church for being a vessel for God and connecting me to Dr. Michael Downey from St. John's Seminary.

Special thanks to Dr. Michael Downey (Editor of the award-winning *The New Dictionary of Catholic Spirituality*) for reading my manuscript and encouraging me to share my book to the world, especially China.

Thanks also to Derek Lin, Taoist master and author of the award-winning *Tao Te Ching: Annotated & Explained*, who offered his friendship and wisdom. I am amazed at his kindness and

Acknowledgments

support for my Christian edition of the Tao Te Ching. It is a miracle how God connected us. (www.dereklin.com)

I offer thanks to Richard, the homeless man who helped me believe both in myself and in this project. The three months I spent with him was a time I would not exchange for anything. I am so blessed by how he helped me understand the power of prayer and by how he gave me the wisdom to understand the Word of God. I don't know where this book would be if it were not for Richard.

I am forever indebted to John Floyd, a business attorney who offered his services to me through my toughest years. John's mentorship was a great blessing. All the professional services I received from his staff brought me much-needed peace. The love John has for others is contagious, and I will keep my promise to pass it on. Thank you, John, for opening your heart and for being a true servant of God. (www.fsklaw.com)

Lin, Derek. *Tao Te Ching: Annotated & Explained*. Woodstock, VT: Skylight Paths Publishing, 2006.